those without shadows

BY

FRANÇOISE SAGAN

BONJOUR TRISTESSE

A CERTAIN SMILE

THOSE WITHOUT SHADOWS

Françoise Sagan

Those Without Shadows

TRANSLATED FROM THE FRENCH

BY FRANCES FRENAYE

E. P. DUTTON & COMPANY, INC.

NEW YORK

1957

DANS UN MOIS DANS UN AN © 1957 by Renè Julliard

Library of Congress Catalog Card Number: 57–12105

those without shadows

those without shadows:

ALAIN: A middle-aged publisher who enjoys the company of young people.

FANNY: Alain's wife, who shares his enthusiasm for youth.

BERNARD: A critic and would-be novelist, married to Nicole but in love with Josée.

NICOLE: Bernard's neglected wife.

JOSÉE: A wealthy girl, who leads an aimless existence while having a love affair with Jacques.

JACQUES: A medical student in love with Josée.

BÉATRICE: An aspiring actress, ex-mistress of Bernard.

JOLYET: A theatrical producer in love with Béatrice.

EDOUARD: Alain's nephew; a pure-hearted young man from the country.

Chapter 1

ERNARD walked into the café, paused for a moment under the gaze of the few customers, whose faces were distorted by the bright neon lights, and went over to the cashier. He liked cashiers: with their well-fed, dignified air, they lived in a dreamy haze punctuated only by small change and matchboxes. This one handed him a telephone slug wearily, without smiling. It was nearly four o'clock in the morning; the booth was dirty and the receiver damp to the touch. As he dialed Josée's number, he realized that his forced, all-night march through Paris had led up to exactly this, to the time when he would be tired enough to make this gesture quite mechanically. It was silly, of course, to call a girl at such an hour. She wouldn't bluntly accuse him of being rude and inconsiderate, but he knew he was acting like a spoiled child, in a way that he inwardly despised. Worse still, he didn't really love Josée; he simply had to know what she was doing. All day long this curiosity obsessed him.

The telephone at the other end was ringing. He leaned against the wall, clutching a package of cigarettes in his pocket. The ringing stopped, and a man's sleepy voice answered: "Hello." Then, a second later, he heard Josée ask: "Who is it?"

Bernard stood stock-still, terrified that she would guess that it was he, that she would catch him trying to surprise her. It was a terrible moment. Finally he pulled the package of cigarettes out of his pocket and hung up the receiver. Next thing he knew, he was walking on the *quais,* along the Seine, muttering to himself one obscenity after another. At the same time a second, hateful voice tried to calm him down: "After all, she's under no obligation to you. You didn't ask anything of her; she's rich and free; you're not her official lover." But already he foresaw a new flood of restless torment, a repeated urge to telephone, an obsession that would continue to haunt the better part of the days to follow. He had played at being a young man, he had talked to Josée about life and books, and spent one night with her, all in a worldly, detached fashion that harmonized with her surroundings. Now he was going home to find the bad novel he was writing strewn over his desk and, in his bed, his wife, sleeping. At this hour she was always asleep, with her childish, fair-skinned face turned toward the door, as if she were afraid he would never come in, waiting for him all night long just as anxiously as she waited through the day.

*   *   *

The young man put down the receiver, and Josée strove to repress the sudden anger she had felt when he had picked it up and answered her telephone as if it were his own.

"I don't know who it was," he said glumly. "He hung up."

"How do you know it was a 'he'?" Josée asked.

"Only a man would call a woman at this hour and then hang up," he said, yawning.

She looked at him curiously, wondering why he was there. How could she have let him bring her home from dinner at Alain's house and then come all the way upstairs? He was handsome enough, but utterly commonplace and uninteresting, far less intelligent than Bernard, and in some ways less attractive, too. Now he sat up on the bed and reached for his watch.

"Four o'clock," he said. "That's a filthy hour."

"What's filthy about it?"

He did not answer, but turned to look at her over his shoulder. She returned his stare and then tried to pull the sheet up around her but arrested the gesture halfway. She knew perfectly well what he was thinking. He had brought her home, made love to her, quite brutally, and then fallen asleep at her side. Now he could look at her quite undisturbed, caring little about what she was or what she might be thinking. At this precise moment she was his. And in the face of this assurance, she was not angry, or even annoyed; she simply felt very humble.

He raised his eyes and gravely ordered her to let go of the sheet. She dropped it, and he stared at her harder than before. She was ashamed, unable either to move or to make the casual remark with which she would have thrown herself down on her stomach in the presence of Bernard, or anyone else, for that matter. This man wouldn't have understood or thought it was funny. He had already made up his mind about her, and nothing could change his elementary, set idea. Her heart was pounding. "I'm lost," she said to herself, but with a feeling of triumph. He leaned toward her with a mysterious smile, and she watched him draw near without blinking.

"The telephone may as well serve some purpose," he said, and fell upon her brusquely. She closed her eyes.

"I'll never be able to make a joke of it again," she reflected. "From now on it won't be the same lighthearted, nighttime affair as before. It will be linked to that look, to something in his face. . . . "

❖   ❖   ❖

"Are you awake?"

Fanny Maligrasse groaned.

"It's my asthma. Be a good boy, will you, Alain, and get me a cup of tea?"

12

Alain Maligrasse hoisted himself out of the other twin bed and wrapped a bathrobe painstakingly about him. For a long period before the war, Alain and Fanny Maligrasse had been a handsome and devoted couple. After four years of separation they had found each other radically changed and bearing the signs of the half-century mark, which they had both attained, upon them. By a touchingly tacit accord they tried to conceal the ravages of the years from each other. At the same time they had taken up the company of the young. The Maligrasses were spoken of, appreciatively, as being fond of young people, and for once the appreciation was deserved. They were not looking for amusement, or for occasions to give good advice; it was simply that they found young people more interesting than those their own age. Neither one of them hesitated to translate feeling into action, when an opportunity arose. Young bodies, no less than young spirits, were attractive to them.

Five minutes later Alain placed a tray on his wife's bed. He looked, not without pity, at the traces of insomnia on her thin, tense face. Only the piercing, dazzlingly gray-blue eyes were as beautiful as ever.

"I think it was a good party," she said, picking up her cup. Alain watched the tea go down her slightly wrinkled throat and let his thoughts wander. Then, making an effort to be responsive, he said:

"I don't understand why Bernard always comes without his wife. Of course I must admit that Josée is terribly attractive."

13

"So's Béatrice, for that matter," Fanny retorted, laughing.

Alain joined in her mirth. His admiration for Béatrice was a standing joke between them, and his wife could not know how cruelly pointed the joke had become. Every Monday night, after what they called their "Monday at-home," he went to bed trembling all over. Béatrice was beautiful and passionate; every time he thought of her these two adjectives imposed themselves upon him and he said them over and over. "Beautiful and passionate," that was Béatrice, hiding her somber, tragic mask when she laughed, because laughter didn't become it; Béatrice talking angrily about her profession because she was not yet successful in it; Béatrice being a little silly, as Fanny called her. Silly? Yes, she was silly, but in a lyrical manner. Alain had worked for twenty years in a publishing house; he was cultivated, underpaid and extremely attached to his wife. How could the standing joke about Béatrice have become a heavy weight that he had to lift when he got up every morning and carry all week until Monday? For on Mondays Béatrice came to their "at-home," where he played the role of the subtle, witty, absent-minded, middle-aged literary man. He loved Béatrice, that was a fact.

"Béatrice is hoping to get a small part in X's next play," said Fanny. ". . . Were there enough sandwiches to go around?"

The Maligrasses were hard put to it to finance their

14

entertaining. The postwar vogue of whisky had nearly wrecked their budget.

"Yes, I think there were," said Alain, who was still sitting on the edge of the bed with his hands dangling between his bony knees. Fanny looked at him with a mixture of tenderness and pity.

"Your little cousin from Normandy is arriving tomorrow," she said. "Here's hoping he has a pure heart, a noble soul, and Josée falls in love with him."

"Josée isn't falling in love with anybody," said Alain. "Couldn't we have some more sleep?"

He took the tray from his wife's knees, planted a kiss on her forehead, and went back to bed. Although the heat was on, he involuntarily shivered. He was an old man, shivering with cold, and not all the literature in the world could help him.

❖　❖　❖

> A month will come, a year will come, and we,
> We shall be parted by a world of seas.
> How shall we suffer when the day begins
> And the sun climbs the sky and then declines,
> And Titus will not see his Berenice . . .　'

Béatrice stood in her dressing gown, looking at herself in the mirror, and the verses dropped from her mouth like stone flowers. "Where did I last read that Racine? . . ." She was overwhelmed by infinite sorrow and at the same time by healthy indignation. She had said these lines a

15

a good many times in the last five years, first for her former husband, and more recently for the benefit of her mirror. And she wished she were before the dark, foaming sea of a theater audience, saying no more than: "Dinner is served," if that was really all there was for her to say.

"I'd do anything in the world for that," she confided to her reflection in the mirror, and the reflection smiled back.

❋ ❋ ❋

At this same moment, the cousin from Normandy, young Edouard Maligrasse, was getting into the train that was to bring him to Paris.

Chapter 2

OR the tenth time that morning Bernard got up from his chair and went to look out the window. He couldn't go on. Writing was humiliating, and what he was writing just now particularly humiliated him. Reading over the last pages, he found them unbearably futile. There was nothing in them of what he wanted to say, nothing of that peculiar essence of things of which he felt he had an intermittent perception. Bernard made a living by writing critical notes for magazines and by reading manuscripts for the literary supplements of various newspapers, as well as for the publishing house where Alain was an editor. Three years before, he had published a novel which the reviewers had found dull but "psycho-logically accurate." He wanted two things: to write a good book, and, more recently, to possess Josée. But words continued to betray him, and Josée had disappeared, captured, no doubt, by one of those sudden fancies for some other country or some new young man—you could never tell which it would be—which her father's fortune and her personal charm allowed her to indulge without deliberation.

"No luck?"

Nicole spoke from just behind him. He had told her from the start to leave him alone with his work, but she couldn't help coming in continually, under the pretext that the morning was the only time she could see him. He knew deep down in his heart, but wouldn't admit it, that the sight of him was absolutely essential to her, and that after more than three years she was more in love with him every day. There was something monstrous about it, because she had long since ceased to attract him. All he cared for was to look back at the picture of himself when he had been in love, at the unexpected decisiveness with which he had made up his mind to marry her. This step seemed to have exhausted his power of decision, for he had taken no demanding step of any kind since.

"No luck at all. And after the poor start I've made there's not much likelihood I'll ever have any."

"But you *will!* I'm quite sure you will."

That tender optimism of hers was the most annoying thing of all. If it had come from Josée, or from Alain, he might have been heartened. But Josée knew nothing about such things, and said so quite frankly, while Alain, although he was encouraging enough, insisted upon handling literature with gloves on. "The really important thing is what you see afterward," he would say. What in the world did he mean? Bernard pretended to understand, but all such hogwash got on his nerves. "Writing takes a pen, a sheet of paper and, to start with, just the shadow of an idea," as Fanny put it. He liked Fanny. He liked them all, and he liked nobody. Josée was supremely irritating but he had to have her. It was enough to kill oneself over.

Nicole was still there. She was putting things in order, puttering around. That was all she did with her lonely days in the apartment. She knew nothing of Paris, nothing of the world of books; she admired both but they frightened her. Only Bernard could have unlocked these worlds for her, but Bernard was out of her range. He was more intelligent, more attractive; people sought after him. And for the present she could not have a baby. She knew nothing beyond Rouen and her father's pharmacy. Bernard had told her so one day, and then begged her to forgive him. At such times he was weak as a child, on the verge of tears. But she preferred such an outburst of deliberate cruelty to the cruelty he showed every day, when he took leave of her with a distracted kiss, immediately after lunch, and didn't come home until late at night. Bernard, even with his restlessness, had always seemed to her a marvelous prize. There are risks in marrying a prize. She couldn't hold that against him.

Now, looking at her, Bernard saw that she was quite pretty, and quite sad.

"Do you want to come with me to the Maligrasses' this evening?" he said gently.

"I'd love to."

Suddenly she looked so happy that Bernard was stricken by remorse. But his remorse was so old and worn by now that he no longer lingered over it. There was no risk in taking her with him, since Josée wouldn't be there. Josée wouldn't have paid any attention to him if she had walked in and found him there with his wife. Or else she would have talked all evening to Nicole. She was capable of such deceptive kindness, not knowing that it was thrown away.

"I'll come for you around nine o'clock," he said. "What are you doing today?" And then, since he knew perfectly well that she had no answer, he added: "See if you can look over this manuscript for me. I'm never going to find the time."

He knew that the request was entirely pointless. Nicole had such respect for the written word, such admiration for any intellectual work, no matter how inept it might be, that she could exercise no critical judgment whatsoever. Of course she would make a tremendous effort to do what he asked, in the hope of making herself useful to him.

"She'd like to be indispensable; that's what every woman wants. . . ." In a mirror in the downstairs hall he caught sight of his angry expression and was ashamed. It was all a frightful mess.

When he reached the publishing house, he found Alain in a state of excitement.

"Béatrice just called up; she wants you to call her back right away."

Bernard had had a somewhat stormy affair with Béatrice, just after the war, and he treated her with a sort of condescending tenderness which left Alain gaping.

"Bernard?" Béatrice spoke in her most important tone of voice; Bernard found it overemphatic. "Bernard, do you know X? Don't you people publish his plays?"

"I know him slightly."

"Fanny heard him mention my name in connection with his next play. I've simply got to meet him. Arrange that for me, Bernard, will you?"

There was something in her tone that reminded Bernard of the palmiest days of their youth, just after the war, when both of them had just escaped from their conventional families and were looking for a hundred francs to pay for their next meal. Once, in that same tone, Béatrice had bullied the notoriously thieving proprietor of a certain bar into advancing them a thousand francs. Such magnetic will power had become a rare thing.

"All right, I'll arrange it. I'll call you again toward the end of the afternoon."

"Call me at five," said Béatrice firmly. "I love you, Bernard. I've always loved you."

"For two years," said Bernard with a laugh.

Still laughing, he wheeled around and caught the expression on Alain's face. Béatrice's voice had carried across the room. Turning quickly back to the telephone, he added:

"Good. I'll see you tonight at Alain's, won't I?"

"Of course."

"He's right here. Do you want to speak to him?" Bernard didn't know exactly why he had raised the question.

"No, I haven't time just now. Tell him I send my love."

Alain's hand was half outstretched to take the receiver. Without looking around, Bernard could see it, the carefully manicured nails and the veins standing out on the skin.

"I'll tell him," he said.

The hand fell, but Bernard paused for a second before turning around.

"She sends you her love," he said at last. "Somebody was there waiting."

He felt miserably unhappy.

*   *   *

Josée stopped her car in front of the Maligrasse house, on the rue de Tournon. The street lamp shone down on its dust-covered hood and the mosquitoes sticking to the windshield.

22

"I don't think I'll go in with you," said the young man. "I haven't anything to say to those people. I'll go study."

Josée was both relieved and disappointed. The week they had spent together in the country had been a bit too much for her. He was either stubbornly quiet or excessively on the go. And his almost vulgar way of taking things for granted held terror as well as fascination.

"I'll come to your house later on, after I've finished working," he said. "Don't be too late getting home."

"I can't tell when I'll be back," said Josée rebelliously.

"Well, make up your mind and tell me right now. It's no use my going so far for nothing, when I haven't a car."

She couldn't tell what he was thinking. She laid her hand on his shoulder.

"Jacques . . ."

He looked coolly into her eyes. She ran her hand around his face, and he wrinkled his forehead.

"Do you like me . . . that way?" he said, with a little laugh.

"Funny," Josée thought. "He must think he's really got under my skin. Jacques F . . . , medical student, my hero. . . . It's all very amusing. It isn't even a physical question, really. I don't know whether it's the reflection of myself that he sends back to me, or the absence of such a reflection or his own personality. . . . But he's fundamentally uninteresting. I doubt if he's even cruel. He exists, that's the most you can say for him."

"Yes, I like you well enough . . . that way," she said. "It's not the passion of a lifetime, yet, but . . ."

"There are such passions," he said gravely.

"Lord help us!" she reflected. "He must be in love with some fair-haired, ethereal young girl. Don't tell me I'm jealous!"

"Do you know from experience?' she asked.

"Not I, but a friend of mine."

She burst out laughing, and he looked at her, wondering whether he ought to be angry. Then he laughed, too, but without gaiety, in a hoarse, almost resentful manner.

✽   ✽   ✽

Béatrice made a triumphal entrance into the Maligrasse drawing room, and even Fanny was struck by her beauty. Nothing becomes some women more than the prick of ambition. Love, on the contrary, may make them very dull. Alain Maligrasse stepped hastily forward to meet her and kissed her hand.

"Is Bernard here?" she asked. Her eyes sought among the dozen people in the room for Bernard; she was ready to trample Alain relentlessly in her search for him. He drew back, while the joyful anticipation written on his face turned to a grimace. Bernard was sitting on a couch, with his wife and a strange young man. In spite of her haste, Béatrice recognized Nicole and felt a stab of compassion. Nicole was sitting very straight, with her hands on her

24

knees and a timid smile on her face. "I'll have to teach her how to live," thought Béatrice in a wave of what she took for benevolence.

"Bernard," she said, "you're really too disgusting. Why didn't you call me up at five o'clock? I rang you at the office a dozen times.... Good evening, Nicole."

"I went to see X," said Bernard triumphantly. "We're to have a drink together, the three of us, at six o'clock tomorrow."

Béatrice sank down on the couch, nearly crushing the strange young man. She had started to apologize when Fanny came up.

"Béatrice, I don't think you know Alain's cousin, Edouard Maligrasse."

Béatrice smiled, really seeing him for the first time. There was something irresistible, something youthful and extraordinarily kind about his face. He stared at her with such astonishment that she couldn't help laughing, and Bernard joined in.

"What's wrong with me?" she asked. "Is it my hair, or do I look like a madwoman?"

Béatrice liked to be thought mad. But just now she was well aware that the young man thought she was very beautiful.

"You don't look at all like a madwoman," he told her. "I'm frightfully sorry if you imagined . . ."

He seemed so embarrassed that she turned away, feeling

ill at ease herself. Bernard looked at her and smiled, while the young man got up and went into the dining room.

"He's simply crazy about you," said Bernard.

"Look here, you're the one who's crazy. I've only just arrived." But she was already convinced that it was true. Without being vain about it, she found it easy to believe that a man was crazy about her.

"It's the sort of thing that happens only in novels, but then he could have stepped right out of a novel's pages," said Bernard. "He's just come to Paris; he's never been really in love, and says so, despairingly. But he'll know a different kind of despair, soon. Our beautiful Béatrice will make him suffer."

"I want to hear about X," Béatrice interrupted. "Is he a fairy?"

"Béatrice, you're too clairvoyant, by far!"

"That's not it," said Béatrice. "But I don't get along with that kind. Fairies are a bore. I like only healthy people."

"I don't know any fairies," put in Nicole.

"Well," said Bernard, "there are three of them right here . . ."

But he stopped abruptly, because Josée had just come into the room. She was laughing with Alain, at the door, and casting occasional glances inside. There were shadows under her eyes and she looked tired. She had not seen him, and he was stricken with a dull pain.

"Josée, where have you been?" Béatrice called out, and

Josée turned and came over to the couch, smiling a little. She looked both exhausted and happy. At the age of twenty-five, she still had that roving, adolescent air which made her spiritually akin to Bernard.

He got up. "I don't think you know my wife," he said. "Josée Saint-Gilles."

Josée smiled, unblinking, kissed Béatrice, and sat down. Bernard stood in front of them, balancing on one leg. All he could think was: "Where has she been? What was she up to during these last ten days? If only she didn't have that money!"

"I've been in the country," she said. "The leaves were turning."

"You look tired," said Bernard.

"I wish *I* could go to the country," said Nicole, glancing at her sympathetically. Josée was the only one of the group who did not intimidate her. Josée was not intimidating until you knew her very well; then her amiability was the kiss of death.

"Do you like the country?" Josée asked her.

"There she goes!" Bernard thought furiously. "Paying attention to Nicole, making herself agreeable. . . . 'Do you like the country,' indeed! Poor Nicole, she probably imagines she's found a friend." And he made for the bar, resolving to get himself plastered.

Nicole looked after him, and Josée felt a mixture of annoyance and pity. She had been mildly curious about Bernard, but he had already proved to be too much like herself, too unstable for her to attach herself to him. And apparently he felt the same way. She tried to answer Nicole, but she was bored, she was tired, and all these people seemed to her lifeless. Her absence had been longer than she thought; she felt as if she had returned from a journey to the land of absurdity.

" . . . and since I don't know anyone who owns a car," Nicole was saying, "I can't ever go for long walks in the woods." And she added brusquely: "Not that I know anyone who *doesn't* own a car, either."

Josée was struck by the bitterness of this last sentence.

"Are you very much alone?" she asked.

"Oh no," said Nicole, quickly retreating; "I was just talking. And besides, I do like the Maligrasses."

Josée hesitated. Three years earlier she would have questioned the woman and tried to help her. But now she was tired, tired of herself and the life she was leading. What was the meaning of this drawing room, or of the brutal young man she had left outside? She knew now that there was no use looking for the answer to a question; the only thing was to wait until the question no longer arose.

"If you like, the next time I go for a drive, I'll pick you up and take you along," she said simply.

Bernard had achieved his purpose: he was slightly drunk and found himself enjoying the conversation of young Maligrasse, although under other circumstances its direction would have vastly annoyed him.

"You say that her name is Béatrice and she's on the stage?

What show is she in? I'll go and see her tomorrow. It's important for me to know her. I've written a play, and she seems to fit the leading role."

Edouard Maligrasse spoke so ardently that Bernard couldn't help laughing.

"You haven't written a play," he answered. "You're just getting ready to fall in love with Béatrice. My friend, that means you're going to suffer. Béatrice is very lovely, but her mainspring is ambition."

"Bernard, don't speak ill of Béatrice on an evening when she particularly adores you," interposed Fanny. "And besides, I'd like you to listen to that boy's playing." And she pointed to a young man who was just settling down at the piano.

Bernard went to sit at the feet of Josée. He felt free and easy in his movements and glad to be alive. He would talk to Josée. "My dear Josée," he would say, "it's a frightful nuisance, but I love you." And this would doubtless be true. Suddenly he remembered the way she had put her arms around his neck the first time he had kissed her, in the library of her apartment, the manner in which she had snuggled up against him. The blood flowed back into his veins. She must surely love him.

The pianist was playing what seemed like a very fine piece of music, very tender, with a certain light theme that recurred over and over, music that had a bowed head. Suddenly Bernard knew what he must write and how he must develop it. The theme was everyman's Josée, the embodiment of youth and youth's most melancholy desires. "That's it!" he thought excitedly. "It's all in that brief theme. Ah, Proust! Yes, Proust has done it already. What good is Proust to me?" He took Josée's hand, but she drew it away. Nicole was looking at him, and because he was fond of her, he shot her a smile.

❋   ❋   ❋

Edouard Maligrasse was a pure-hearted young man. He did not mistake vanity for love, and he aspired to have only genuine passions. Having been starved of such things at Caen, he came to Paris like a disarmed conqueror, without the aim of making big money or owning a sports car or enjoying any particular group's esteem. His father had found him a small job with an insurance agent, which he had held now for a whole week, with genuine satisfaction. He enjoyed the rear platforms of the buses, the cafés where one stood at a bar, and the smiles that the women tossed in his direction. There was something captivating about him; it was not so much his innocence as his complete availability.

Béatrice had inspired him with an immediate passion, a violent desire, such as his one-time mistress, the wife of a Caen notary, had never awakened. She had walked into the Maligrasse drawing room with all the aura of the world of fashion and the theater about her. And her ambition was a sentiment which he could admire, even without understanding. The day would come when Béatrice would

30

throw back her head and say: "I care more for you than for my career," and he would bury his face in her black hair and silence the tragic mask of her face with a kiss. He said all these things to himself, over a glass of lemonade, while the young man played the piano. Bernard seemed to be a fine fellow; he had the eager and yet sardonic manner of the Parisian journalists he had read about in Balzac.

At the end of the evening Edouard rushed forward to offer to take Béatrice home. But she had come in a small car, borrowed from a friend, and proposed, instead, that she drop him off on her way.

"I might go with you and then walk back," he suggested.

But she insisted that this was quite unnecessary, and set him down at the unattractive corner of the boulevard Haussmann and the rue Tronchet, not far from his lodgings. He looked so helpless that she brushed his cheek with her hand and said: "Good-by, young goat." She loved discovering that people resembled animals, and besides, this goat seemed quite ready to enter the temporarily empty stable of her admirers. He was a handsome fellow, and now he was obviously fascinated by the hand which she had thrust out through the car window. Like an animal at bay, he breathed heavily, and in a moment of emotion she gave him her telephone number, much sooner than was her wont after a first meeting. From then on the name of "Elysées," her telephone exchange, became for Edouard the symbol of his Parisian progress. The sad procession of all the other exchanges, including "Danton" (Maligrasse) and

"Wagram" (insurance office), followed a long way behind. He walked on air through the Paris streets, in true lover's fashion, while Béatrice recited the tirade from Racine before her mirror. It was a superb exercise, and the road to success is paved with discipline and hard work, as everyone knows.

Chapter 3

THE first meeting between Jacques and those whom, for nearly a month now, Josée had secretly called "the others," was charged with pain. She had hidden him from them, not without difficulty, for she felt sorely tempted to break part of her ties with their little group, the part based upon good taste, mutual fondness and esteem—the part which made these people admire one another, whereas they could understand Jacques only by mistakenly attributing to her affair a purely sexual motivation. Only Fanny was capable of understanding, and it was to her that Josée resolved that she would first reveal the relationship between them. She went

33

for tea at the house on the rue de Tournon and asked Jacques to call there for her. He had told her that his presence in the Maligrasse drawing room on the evening when they had first met was a matter of pure chance; he had been brought by one of Béatrice's admirers. "In fact, you nearly missed me," he had added; "I was bored stiff and just on the point of leaving." She didn't ask why he hadn't said "I nearly missed you," or "We nearly missed each other." Because Jacques always spoke of his existence in relation to other people as an accident—whether happy or not, he failed to say—which descended upon them. In her own case, Josée had come to the conclusion that it was happy. He *was* an accident, no doubt of that, and already she was tired of it. But nothing—neither boredom nor annoyance—was yet strong enough to match the curiosity she still felt about him.

Fanny was all alone and reading a new novel. She always read the latest fiction, but never quoted anyone except Flaubert or Racine, because she had a keen sense of what one should be impressed by. She and Josée were good friends; at times they puzzled each other, but there was a tacit confidence between them which no one else could share. They spoke first of Edouard's passion for Béatrice, and the role she had obtained in X's play.

"She'll be better in X's production than in the one she's about to play with poor Edouard," Fanny remarked.

She was tiny, and distinguished by her gracious movements and beautifully kept hair. The mauve sofa was becoming to her, and so were the other pieces of English furniture in the room.

"You harmonize with your apartment, Fanny," Josée told her. "I think that's something quite unusual."

"Who decorated yours?" Fanny asked. "Oh yes, it was Levêgue, and he did a very good job, didn't he?"

"I don't know. So people say. I don't think it really becomes me. I seldom feel in harmony with interior decoration of any kind. Only sometimes with people."

She thought of Jacques, and reddened. Fanny shot her a glance.

"You're blushing. I think you have too much money, Josée. What's happened to your courses at the Ecole du Louvre? And how are your parents?"

"You know perfectly well what sort of pretext the Ecole du Louvre is to me. . . . My parents are still in North Africa, and they still send me checks. I'm completely useless, from a sociological point of view I don't really care, but . . ." She hesitated before going on. "I do wish there were something I could do with enjoyment, no, with passion . . ." She stopped again, and then said brusquely:

"What about you?"

Fanny Maligrasse opened her eyes wide in a comic fashion.

"Me?"

"Yes. You're always the listener. Let's exchange roles . . . unless I'm being indiscreet."

"No," said Fanny, laughing. "*I* have Alain Maligrasse."

Josée raised her eyebrows, and in the silence that followed they looked at each other as if they were the same age.

"Is it that easy to see?" asked Fanny.

Josée was touched and embarrassed by her tone of voice. Fanny rose and began to walk up and down the room.

"I don't know what there is about Béatrice. Is it her beauty? Or that blind force? She's the only one of us who has any real ambition."

"How about Bernard?"

"Bernard cares for books more than anything else. It's not at all the same thing. And then he's intelligent. There's nothing like a certain kind of stupidity."

Josée thought again of Jacques. She decided to speak to Fanny about him, although originally she had wanted to see Fanny's surprise when he arrived unexpectedly. But just then Bernard came in. His face lit up with pleasure at the sight of Josée, and this Fanny did not fail to notice.

"Fanny, your spouse has to go to a business dinner, and because he won't have time to come home, he's dispatched me to bring him his most handsome tie. 'The blue one with black stripes,' that's how he described it."

All three of them laughed, and while Fanny went to look for the tie, Bernard clasped Josée's hands.

"Josée, I'm happy to see you. But sorry that it's always so briefly. Can't you find time to have dinner with me?"

Josée looked at him. She detected a mixture of joy and bitterness in his air. He had bright eyes, black hair, and held his head slightly inclined. "He's like me," she thought. "We belong to the same breed. I should have loved him."

"We can have dinner together whenever you say," she answered.

For the past fortnight she had dined every night with Jacques in her apartment. He didn't want to take her to a restaurant, where he couldn't pick up the check, and this arrangement salved his pride. After dinner he did some intensive cramming while Josée read a book. She was used to staying out late and hearing amusing conversation, and this sort of conjugal life with a semimute companion was something quite extraordinary. All of a sudden she realized *how* extraordinary it was. Then the front-door bell rang and she freed herself from Bernard's hands.

"Someone's asking for the young lady," said the maid.

"Show him in," said Fanny, appearing at the other door of the room. Bernard had turned to look into the hall. "We might be on the stage," Josée thought, starting to giggle.

Jacques made an entrance like that of a bull into an arena, holding his head low and tapping the rug with one foot. He had a Belgian name, and as Josée began stumblingly to pronounce it, Jacques interrupted:

"I've come to get you," he said.

He kept his hands in his duffle-coat pocket with a threatening air. "He's quite, quite impossible," thought Josée, stifling her giggle, but not before experiencing a moment of joy at the sight of him and also at the look on Fanny's face. Bernard wore a completely inscrutable expression, as if he had suddenly become blind.

"You might at least say hello," said Josée, almost tenderly. Jacques smiled, somewhat appealingly, and shook Fanny's and Bernard's hands. The setting sun on the rue de Tournon brought out the reddishness of his hair. "There's a word for men of this kind," thought Josée. "Vital, virile . . . ?"

"There's a word to describe this kind of boy," Fanny was simultaneously thinking. "A boor, that's what he is. But where have I seen him before? Was it here?"

Vaguely she remembered, and made herself agreeable to him.

"Sit down, won't you? Why should we all be standing? Will you have some tea, or are you in too much of a hurry?"

"No, I have time," said Jacques. And looking at Josée, he added: "How about you?"

Josée nodded.

"I must be going," said Bernard.

"I'll come to the door with you, Bernard," said Fanny. "You're forgetting the tie."

He was already in the entrance hall, looking very pale. Fanny had meant to exchange signs of astonishment with him, but now she did not make a single gesture. He went away without saying a word and Fanny returned to the drawing room. Jacques was sitting down, looking at Josée with a broad smile.

"I'm betting that was the man on the telephone," he said.

✳   ✳   ✳

Bernard walked down the street mumbling to himself like one possessed. Finally he found a bench, sat down, and threw his arms around his body, as if he were cold. "Josée," he thought, "Josée and that little brute!" He swayed back and forth under the impulse of a real physical pain, until an old woman sitting nearby looked at him with amazement and a beginning of terror. When he saw that he had drawn her attention, he got up and resumed his walking. He simply had to take Alain his tie.

"This is quite enough," he said to himself resolutely. "It's intolerable. Bad novels . . . this ridiculous passion for a little slut. She isn't even a slut, and I don't really love her; I'm jealous, that's all. It can't go on this way; it's too much, or too little." At the same instant he reached a decision to go away. "I can find a cultural mission of some kind," he thought bitterly. "That's all I'm good for, cultural missions, cultural talks, little cultural pieces in the papers. When you don't really know how to do anything, you can always fall back on exploiting culture." And what about Nicole? He'd send her back to her mother for a month and try to get hold of himself. But how could he bear to leave Paris and . . . Josée? Meanwhile, where would she go with this boy, what would she do? . . . On the stairs he bumped into Alain.

"At last, my tie!" Alain exclaimed.

He was to dine with Béatrice, before the play. Since

she didn't come on until the second act, they would have until ten o'clock. Every minute of their tête-à-tête seemed inestimably precious to him. He had told Béatrice he wanted to talk to her about his nephew, Edouard. This was the first excuse he had ever found for seeing her outside the Monday-evening at-homes.

* * *

Wearing his new tie, and vaguely worried about the look he had caught on the face of his protégé, Bernard, Alain set out to call for Béatrice at her apartment, on a narrow street near the avenue Montaigne. He imagined . . . well, he didn't know exactly what he imagined . . . Béatrice and himself in a quietly luxurious restaurant, the noise of traffic outside and, above all, what he called her "admirable mask," veiled by the dim light of a rose-shaded lamp, leaning toward him. He was Alain Maligrasse, a tall man (he knew that was important in Béatrice's eyes), of impeccable tastes, slightly blasé. They would talk, first indulgently and then with a certain boredom, about Edouard, and then they would pass on to the subject of life in general, to the disillusionment which life inevitably brings to beautiful women. . . . He would hold her hand on the table; no bolder gesture came to mind. But Béatrice's attitude remained a complete unknown. He was slightly apprehensive, because he foresaw that she would be afflicted with the radiancy and good cheer that come with ambition.

40

As it turned out, Béatrice was playing a role that might very well have harmonized with his. A few kind words from the director of X's play and the unexpected attentions of an influential dramatic critic had pushed her thoughts onto one of those paths which the imagination follows so precipitately when there is the least impetus from the outside world, a path leading in this case to an artistic triumph. And so, this evening, she was a young and successful actress. And, thanks to some miracle of sentimental compromise which only petty souls can achieve, she chose to be the triumphant young actress who values the conversation of a literary man above the more sophisticated pleasures of a night club. After all, success does not preclude originality. And so she inveigled Alain Maligrasse, who had carefully worked out a way to be extravagant, into a so-called intellectual hole in the wall. Here there was no rose lampshade between them, but rather the hurried hands of an unpolished waitress, the clatter of the other tables, and the sound of a vile guitar.

"My dear Alain," Béatrice said in her deep voice, "what's going on? I must say that your telephone call greatly intrigued me."

X's play was a historical detective drama.

"It's about Edouard," Maligrasse said nervously.

Time was going by, and he sat there, molding his bread with his fingers. The first half-hour had been a hurly-burly of taxis, Béatrice's contradictory instructions to the driver as to how to find this infamous spot, and supplications to

41

the proprietor to give them a table. He would have liked a minute to breathe. Worst of all, there was a mirror just across from him, in which he could discern his long, slightly sagging face, wrinkled in some spots and childishly smooth in others. There are people whom life marks quite at random with the signs of an uncertain old age. He sighed.

"Edouard?" said Béatrice, with a questioning smile.

"Yes, Edouard." Her smile stabbed at his heart. "What I say may seem ridiculous to you"—God grant it does!—"but Edouard is only a child. He's in love with you, and since his arrival he's borrowed more than a hundred thousand francs, fifty thousand of them from Josée, and spent them on outrageously expensive suits, all in order to meet your approval."

"He's been overwhelming me with flowers," said Béatrice, smiling again.

It was a perfectly constructed smile, eloquent of slightly weary indulgence, but because Alain went very seldom to see moving pictures or bad plays, he did not recognize it as such and took it as a sign that she returned Edouard's love. All at once he wanted to go away.

"How tiresome!" he said weakly.

"Tiresome that someone should be in love with me?" said Béatrice, lowering her head as if to turn away from the conversation. But Alain's heart was leaping.

"I understand it all too well," he said fervently, and Béatrice stifled a laugh.

42

"I'll have some cheese," she said. "Tell me more about Edouard. I must admit he amuses me. But I don't like the idea of his borrowing money."

For a moment she had wanted to exclaim: "Let him go ahead and ruin himself! What other use is a very young man?" But aside from the fact that she was too kindhearted really to feel that way, she realized that it was not at all what an alarmed uncle would want to hear. And there *was* an alarmed look about Alain. She leaned over, just as he had seen her do in his imagination, while the guitar agonized and the pretentious candles flickered in her eyes.

"What am I to do, Alain? And quite honestly, what *can* I do?"

He caught his breath and launched into a confused explanation. Perhaps she could make it clear to Edouard that there was no use hoping.

"But there *is*," Béatrice thought to herself gaily. She was touched by the thought of Edouard, with his fine, light-brown hair and awkward gestures and the ebullient way he spoke over the telephone. And for her sake he was borrowing money! She forgot the play and her part in it, and suddenly wished she could see Edouard, hold him to her and feel him tremble with happiness. She had seen him only once, in a bar, since their first meeting, and he had stood very stiffly, but with such a dazzled expression that she had felt something like pride. As far as Edouard was concerned, her every gesture was a fabulous gift, and she

43

had a vague feeling that her relationships with other human beings could be only of that order.

"I'll do what I can," she said. "I swear it . . . by my love for Fanny. And you know how devoted I am to her."

"What a little fool!" This reflection crossed Alain's mind, but he stuck to his original plan. Now he would change the subject and lead up to an opportunity of holding Béatrice's hand.

"Let's move on," he proposed. "How about having a drink somewhere else before the second act? I couldn't eat another thing."

"We might go to Vat's," thought Béatrice, "only there one's apt to run into so many people. Of course, Alain does have a certain reputation, but only in a very small circle, and his tie makes him look like a lawyer's clerk. Dear Alain, so old-fashioned!" And she stretched her hand across the table to take the one that Alain extended to her.

"We'll go wherever you say," she said. "I'm happy just because you exist."

Alain wiped his mouth, and in a feeble voice asked for the check. Béatrice patted his hand with hers and then she slipped it into a red glove, which matched her shoes. They had a glass of whisky in a café across the street from the theater and talked about the war years, the postwar years. . . . "The young people of today have no idea what it is to listen to boogie-woogie music in some Left Bank dive," Béatrice was saying. At ten o'clock, when they took

44

leave of each other, Alain had long since given up the struggle. For the last hour he had listened with a somber joy to Béatrice's commonplaces, from time to time summoning up his courage to steal an admiring look at her face. Because she was in such good form, she made a flirtatious gesture or two in his direction, but he didn't even notice them. When a man has dreamed of winning something by a colossal stroke of luck, he is prone to neglect petty but more practical ways of attaining it. Alain Maligrasse had taken less from Balzac than from Stendhal, and his sensibility cost him dear. It cost him the knowledge that what we love we may also despise. He was spared a crisis, no doubt, but a crisis might at least have had something definitive about it. Of course, at his age, passion can more easily dispense with esteem. But he could not, like Josée, find consolation in the blessed tangibility of: "This boy is mine."

He went home like a thief. If he had spent three hours with Béatrice in a hotel, he would have returned triumphantly, his conscience washed clean by happiness. But because he had not been unfaithful to Fanny, after all, he was beset by guilt. Fanny was sitting up in bed, with a blue bed jacket around her. He got undressed in the bathroom, muttering something vague about his business dinner and feeling as if he had been through the mill.

"Good night, Fanny."

He leaned over his wife and she drew his head against her shoulder.

"Of course, she knows," he thought wearily. "But this isn't what I want. I want Béatrice's firm, round shoulder. What I need to see is Béatrice's upturned, delirious face, and not these intelligent eyes that bore through me."

"I'm very unhappy," he said aloud, freeing himself from her embrace and climbing into bed.

Chapter 4

BERNARD was going away, and Nicole was crying, just as he had known she would be, all along. As Bernard packed his bag, it seemed to him that the whole course of his life had been predictable, from the very beginning. It was natural that he should have good looks, a restless youth, a passing affair with Béatrice, and an affair with literature which seemed to have no ending. And still more natural that he should marry this rather insignificant young woman and cause her a deep, animal-like suffering which was totally incomprehensible to him. He was a brute; he had all the petty complexities and cruelties of an average man. Meanwhile, he must play the part of the reassuring male. He turned to Nicole and took her in his arms.

"Don't cry, darling. You know that I've got to get away. It's very important. A month is no time at all, and with your parents . . . "

"I don't want to go back to my parents, even for a month," Nicole said stubbornly.

It was her new obsession. She wanted to stay in this apartment. And he knew that every night she would sleep with her head turned toward the door, waiting. He was overwhelmed by a tremendous pity which he at once extended to himself as well.

"You'll be bored here, all alone."

"I'll go to see the Maligrasses. And Josée promised to take me out in her car."

"Josée!" He let go of her, seized roughly upon his shirts and stuffed them into the suitcase. Josée. Never mind about Nicole and his feeling of human sympathy toward her! Josée. When would he be delivered from this name, this jealousy? The only violent feeling he had ever had in his whole life, and it had to be jealousy. He found himself utterly hateful.

"You'll write, won't you?" Nicole was asking.

"Every day."

He felt like wheeling around and saying: "I could just as easily write all thirty letters in advance."

"Darling —Everything's all right. Italy is wonderful; we'll have to see it together one day. I'm doing the most tremendous amount of work, but I miss you, and you are always in my thoughts. Shall write more tomorrow. Love and kisses." Those were the things he would write to her during the month to come. Why did there have to be some people who inspired you and others who didn't? Ah, Josée! He'd write very differently to *her:* "Josée, if you only knew! I don't know how to make you understand, and I am far away, far from that face of yours whose very memory is painful to me. Josée, am I all wrong, or is there still time?" Yes, he knew exactly how it was going to be; he would write to Josée from Italy, one night when he was in excessively low spirits, and the words would flow, hard and heavy, out of his pen and they would be alive. At last he would find the secret of writing. But Nicole . . . Nicole was blond, and she was still crying, very gently, leaning against his back.

"I'm sorry," he said.

"*I'm* the one to be sorry. I simply can't . . . Oh, Bernard, I've tried, I've tried, very hard . . . "

"You've tried what?" he asked nervously.

"I've tried to live up to you, to keep you company and help you. But I haven't the brains, and I'm not particularly amusing; I've known it all along . . . Oh, Bernard! . . ."

She was choking on her tears. Bernard held her in his arms and begged her forgiveness, over and over, in a lifeless voice.

Next thing he knew he was on the road, in the car which his publisher had lent him, making the motions proper to a man at the wheel. Lighting a cigarette with one hand, noting the play of the headlights on the road before him, the dimming which indicated the fear or friendliness of his fellow drivers, and the way the leafy trees loomed up ahead and then flew by. This was what it was to be alone. He wanted to keep going all night long, and already he recognized the taste of fatigue. A sort of resigned happiness descended upon him. He was a complete failure, perhaps, but what did it matter? There was something else; he'd always sensed it; something about being alone which almost exhilarated him. Tomorrow would belong, once more, to Josée; he would commit a thousand acts of cowardice and suffer a thousand defeats, but this evening, beyond his weariness and sorrow, he had attained this something else which would always be accessible to him, this tranquil image of himself cradled by leafy trees.

Nothing is more like one Italian town than another Italian town, especially in the fall. After spending six days between Milan and Geneva and visiting a fair number of libraries and museums, Bernard decided to go back to France. He longed for a hotel room in some French provincial town. He chose Poitiers, which seemed to him the deadest town that could be found, and hunted up its most commonplace hotel, called L'Ecu de France. This background was deliberately planned, on his part, as if it were a stage setting, reminiscent, at different hours of the day, of Stendhal or Simenon. And yet he did not know what play he would act out against it, what failure or false discovery awaited him. All he knew was that he would be deliberately bored, and probably despairing, and that his boredom and despair, if carried far enough, might get him out of the morass in which he had foundered. After ten days in the car he realized that the morass was not his passion for Josée, his failure to write a good book, or his weariness of Nicole. It was something lacking in this passion, this failure, this weariness, something to fill the vacancy he felt when he woke up every morning, to overcome his self-irritation. Now he was laying down his arms and surrendering to the monster. For three weeks he would have to put up with himself, quite alone.

The first day he reconnoitered and set up the ports of call of his itinerary: the newspaper stand, the Café du Commerce, where he would drink an *apéritif*, the little restaurant on the other side of the square, and the moving-picture theater on the corner. His hotel room was decorated with blue and gray wallpaper bearing a design of large faded flowers; the washstand was enameled and the bedside rug dark brown. Everything was in keeping. From the window he could see the house across the way, plastered with a tattered advertisement for "The House of the Hundred Thousand Shirts." It had a closed window whose opening might furnish him with a vague, romantic hope. His table was covered with a white cloth which had a tendency to slip off to one side and had to be removed so that he could write. The proprietress of the hotel was welcoming, but in a reserved fashion, the chambermaid old and talkative. Finally, it was raining a lot in Poitiers that year. Bernard unpacked and arranged his things quite seriously, with no sense of irony. He treated himself with care, as if he were a stranger, bought a large number of newspapers, and, the second day, even allowed himself to drink too many glasses of white wine and *cassis*. These left him in a state of intoxication which was dangerous, inasmuch as it immediately took on the name of Josée. "Waiter, how long would it take me to put through a telephone call to Paris?" But he managed not to make the call.

He resumed work on his novel. The first sentence was a moralistic one: "Happiness is always subject to slander." This statement struck him as exact but completely futile. However, it was enthroned at the top of the page: "Chapter I. Happiness is always subject to slander. Jean-Jacques was a happy man, and people spoke ill of him." Actually, he would have preferred another beginning: "The little village of Boissy seems to the passing traveler's eye a peaceful spot, where the sun . . . " But he couldn't make such a slow start; he must go right to essentials. But what *were* essentials, and what was this idea about essentials, anyway? Every morning he wrote for an hour, then went out to buy the newspapers, get himself shaved, and eat his lunch. He worked for three more hours in the afternoon, read for a while (Rousseau), and took a walk before dinner. After that, a moving picture, and once a visit to the local brothel, which was no more sordid than any other and gave him proof that the most jaded appetite can be stimulated by privation.

The second week did not go so well. His novel was bad.

He reread it cold-bloodedly and had to admit it. Actually, it wasn't even bad, it was something worse. It was boring, very boring indeed. He wrote as if he were cutting his nails, half-attentive, half-distracted. Meanwhile, he noted his state of health, the impairment of his liver, and the nervousness of his reflexes, all the minor damages wrought by life in Paris. One afternoon he looked at himself in the bedroom mirror, and went to stand against the wall, pressing himself close to its cold, hard surface with outstretched arms. At a certain point he wrote a laconic but despairing letter to Alain Maligrasse, who wrote back that he should turn away from introspection and look around him. Stupid advice, as Bernard knew. No one ever has time to examine himself honestly, and most people look no further than their neighbors' eyes, in which they may see their own reflection. It was in this state of mind, obscurely hemmed in by his own limitations, that Bernard stood his ground. He had no intention of letting himself escape to the bosom of a woman of Poitiers.

The whole episode, he knew, would lead to nothing but more pain. He would go back to Paris with his nearly finished manuscript under one arm and hand it over to his publisher who would proceed to print it. He would try to see Josée, and to ignore the reproachful look in Nicole's eyes. It was all quite useless, but from his conviction of its uselessness he arrived at a sort of hard-surfaced calm. He foresaw, also, in what humorous terms he would describe the amusements of Poitiers. How he would enjoy the as-

53

tonished look in people's eyes when he told them of this escapade! It would even give him a vague sense of his own originality. With what masculine reserve he would say "I spent most of the time working." He knew in advance how he would stylize and embroider the whole story. But what difference did it make? Through the open window he listened to the sounds of the night and the falling rain, and followed with his eyes the yellow headlights of the occasional passing cars as they played upon the wallpaper's slightly faded roses and then left them once more submerged in shadow. Lying on his back, with his arms crossed beneath his head, his eyes open, Bernard smoked his last cigarette of the day.

* * *

Edouard Maligrasse was not a fool. He was a young man made to be violently happy or unhappy, and for whom indifference would have spelled death. Now he was happy to have found Béatrice and to love her.

Béatrice was astonished by the happiness he found in this passion. Most people consider unreciprocated love a catastrophe, and this disinterestedness was something she had never met before. To astonish Béatrice meant to obtain a two weeks' start, an advantage which Edouard's looks alone would never have assured him. Although she was not cold, Béatrice had little taste for physical love. Still, she thought it was very healthy, and had believed for a short time that she was a woman ruled by her senses, a belief which she made into an excuse for deceiving her husband. Since, in her circle, adultery was not at all difficult, she felt the need of playing a drama of renunciation. Her lover was hurt, and her husband, to whom in climactic Third Act tradition, she had insisted upon telling the whole story, was vastly annoyed. He was a common-sense businessman, and found it utterly ridiculous for Béatrice to say all in one breath that she had a lover but meant to give him up without delay. "She might just as well have kept her mouth shut about it," he reflected, while in a lugubrious monotone Béatrice, minus her make-up, accused herself of her sin.

So now Edouard Maligrasse appeared, radiating happiness, at Béatrice's apartment house, her hairdresser's, and the stage door. He felt quite sure she would love him someday and waited patiently for her to give him what he considered the proof of it. Unfortunately, Béatrice was becoming used to this platonic devotion, and no habit, once acquired, is harder to lose, particularly for a featherheaded woman. One evening, when he brought Béatrice home from the theater, Edouard asked her if he could come upstairs for a drink. Let it be said in his defense that he was not acquainted with the ritual meaning of this request. Talking about love had left him thirsty, and because he had not a penny in his pocket, he faced a dry walk home.

"No, Edouard dear," Béatrice said tenderly. "It's very late, and I think you'd better be on your way."

"You don't know how thirsty I am," Edouard insisted. "I

don't want whisky, just a simple glass of water." And he added chastely: "I'm afraid the cafés may be closed at this late hour."

They looked at each other. The light from the street lamp brought out the delicacy of Edouard's features in a particularly flattering way. It was a chilly evening, and Béatrice surreptitiously enjoyed the prospect of refusing herself in a casual but beautifully staged scene beside a lighted fire. They went upstairs together, and while Edouard lit the kindling, Béatrice prepared a tray. They sat down beside the fireplace and Edouard kissed Béatrice's hand. He had begun to realize that the time and the place were propitious, and he imperceptibly trembled.

"I'm so glad we're friends," Béatrice said dreamily, and he kissed the palm of her hand. "You know," she went on, "in the theatrical world—which I love very dearly, since it is my own—there are so many people . . . well, cynical is too strong a word for them, but they seem to have lost their youth. You are young, Edouard, and I hope you'll remain so for a long time to come."

She spoke in a charmingly grave manner. Edouard Maligrasse felt very young indeed; with blazing cheeks he pressed his lips to her wrist.

"You'd better go now," she said brusquely. "We mustn't . . . I have the most complete trust in you; you know that."

If he had been a few years older, Edouard would have pressed the point home. But his youth saved him. He got up, almost apologetically, and started toward the door.

Béatrice felt that the scene, which she had played with so much style, was slipping away. She was no longer sleepy and the hours ahead promised to be a bore. A single word could save her, and she said it.

"Edouard!"

He turned around.

"Come back."

She stretched out her hands in a gesture of surrender. Edouard held them for a long time in his, then, happily carried away by his youth, he caught her in his arms, searched for her lips and found them. He moaned a little with happiness, for he genuinely loved her. Late that night he was still murmuring words of love, with his head on the sleeping Béatrice's breast. Little did she know what long-unfulfilled dreams had inspired them.

Chapter 5

WAKING up at Béatrice's side, Edouard lived through one of those moments of happiness that seem, at the time, to justify a whole existence, but that the dimmer perception of later years brands as the cause of its perdition. Half asleep, he saw Béatrice's shoulder through his eyelashes, and he was stabbed by memory, that tyrant which impinges upon our dreams and leaps at our throat as soon as we awaken. Blissfully, he stretched out his hand toward Béatrice's naked back. But sleep was indispensable to Béatrice's complexion; along with hunger

and thirst, it was one of the few strictly natural and genuine things in which she indulged. She rolled over to the
far side of the bed, and Edouard found himself alone.

Tender memories still besieged him, but before her re-
lentless retreat he began to guess at the treachery of love,
and he was afraid. His impulse was to turn her over, lean
his head against her shoulder, and give thanks. But faced
by this stubborn back, this triumphant sleep, he contented
himself with reaching across the bedcovers and caressing
her deceivingly generous body with a quickly resigned
hand.

There was something symbolic about this awakening,
but of course Edouard did not see it in that way. He could
not know, at this early stage of the game, that his passion
for Béatrice would amount to nothing more than this: the
contemplation of her back. We make our own symbols,
after the event has passed and begun to spoil. He was not
like Josée, who woke up at the same moment, looked, in
the light of dawn, at the smooth, hard back of her lover,
and smiled before she went back to sleep. But then Josée
was much older than Edouard.

❀   ❀   ❀

From then on, for Béatrice and Edouard, life fell into a
regular pattern. He called for her at the theater every
night, and had lunch with her as often as she would let
him. Béatrice went in for lunching with her women friends,
partly because she had read that it was usual custom in

59

America and partly in the belief that her elders had much to teach her. For this latter reason she often chose the company of old actresses who were jealous of her increasing success. If she had not been made of stone, she would have been pushed into an inferiority complex by the acrimonious character of their observations.

Fame creeps up rather than explodes upon us. Finally something happens to reveal that it is here. In Béatrice's case, this something was the proposal of André Jolyet, well-known gourmet and theatrical producer, that she should play an important part in his forthcoming October show and meanwhile occupy his villa in the south of France while she memorized her role.

Béatrice wanted to consult Bernard. She considered him a "bright boy" in spite of the fact that he had several times denied this distinction. It amazed her to hear that he was at Poitiers. What in the world could he be doing there? Finally she telephoned Nicole.

"I hear Bernard's at Poitiers. What's he up to?"

"I don't know," said Nicole briefly. "He's supposed to be working."

"How long has he been away?"

"Two months," said Nicole, bursting into sobs.

Béatrice was overcome with surprise. She still had something of a kind heart, and at once her imagination pictured Bernard as wildly in love with the wife of the mayor. How else could he endure life in the provinces? She pledged herself to call immediately on poor Nicole, but shortly afterward she received an irresistible invitation from André Jolyet. Not wishing to let Nicole down, she asked Josée to make the call in her place.

Josée was at home, reading. She had never felt completely at ease in her apartment, and the telephone alternately comforted and annoyed her. Béatrice painted the situation in dark colors, and Josée was completely puzzled. Just the day before, she had received a beautifully written letter from Bernard, dissecting his feelings for her; obviously there was no place in his life for a mysterious woman of Poitiers. She promised to go see Nicole, and, being a young woman of her word, proceeded to do so.

The first thing she noticed was that Nicole had put on weight. This is the effect which, in three cases out of four, unhappiness has upon women. The process of eating guarantees at least the health of the body. Josée explained that she had come in Béatrice's place, and since Nicole found Béatrice highly intimidating and regretted having let herself go during their telephone talk, she was greatly relieved by this substitution. Josée was slender, with a mobile, adolescent face and the gestures of a thief. Because Nicole did not guess at her underlying self-sufficiency, she took her to be even more clumsy in her approach to life than herself.

"Shall we go to the country?" Josée asked her.

She had a big American car and drove it fast and skillfully, while Nicole sat hunched up at the other end of the seat. Josée was bored and at the same time pleased with herself for doing a good deed. The letter she had just received from Bernard was fresh in her mind:

> Josée, I love you; it's all very painful. Here I am, trying to work, but I can't do it. My life is a slow whirl, without music. I know you don't love me, and why should you? We're too much alike, and I'm the only one that's incestuous. I'm writing you this only because it doesn't really matter. I mean, it doesn't matter whether I write you or not. That's the only good thing about being alone; one learns to accept oneself and give up a certain kind of vanity. There's that other boy, I know, and of course I don't like him. . . .

Almost every sentence had stuck in her mind. She had read the letter at breakfast, while Jacques was deep in *Le Figaro*, to which her father had given her a subscription. She had put the letter down on the bedside table, feeling that the whole thing was a mess. Jacques had got up, whistling, and remarked, as he did every morning, that the papers were a total waste of time. Why, then, Josée wondered, did he read them with such care? "Perhaps he's murdered some rich old widow," she thought, laughing to herself. After that Jacques had taken a shower and emerged from the bathroom fully dressed and with his duffle coat on, just in time to give her a hasty kiss before going off to his classes. She had wondered how it was she could still put up with him.

"I know a little inn where they have a heavenly open fire," she said now, in order to escape from Nicole's silence.

What else was she to say? "Your husband's in love with

me, but I'm not in love with him; I shan't take him away from you and he'll get over it in the long run." That would have been a betrayal of Bernard's superior intelligence and understanding. And to explain anything to Nicole was like leading a lamb to the slaughter.

At lunch they talked first of Béatrice and then of the Maligrasses. Nicole was positive that they were devoted and faithful to each other, and Josée did not disillusion her on the latter score. She felt weary and benevolent. Nicole was three years older than herself and there was nothing she could do for her. Nothing at all. There is a certain kind of stupidity reserved for women's dealings with men. Little by little, Josée felt Nicole getting on her nerves; she despised her hesitation over the menu and the lost look in her eyes. When the coffee came there was an awkward silence, which Nicole broke by the abrupt statement:

"Bernard and I are going to have a baby."

"But I thought . . . "

She knew that Nicole had had two miscarriages and the doctor had expressly advised her not to try again.

"I wanted it," Nicole added, with lowered head and an obstinate air.

"Does Bernard know?" asked Josée, looking at her in amazement.

"No."

"God help us!" Josée thought. "Here we have one of those regular biblical women! She thinks that a baby will win back her man. And so she doesn't hesitate to put him on the spot. I'll never be a biblical woman myself. But meanwhile, this one must be frightfully unhappy."

"You ought to write to him," she said aloud.

"I don't dare. First, I want to be sure that nothing will go wrong."

"I still think you ought to tell him."

What if it did go wrong again, and Bernard weren't there? . . . Josée paled. She couldn't imagine Bernard as a father. Whereas Jacques . . . yes. . . . She could see Jacques, standing at her bedside, looking faintly embarrassed, and smiling at the sight of his child. But she must be delirious. . . .

"We'd better go home," she said.

She drove slowly all the way. As she turned up the Champs Elysées, Nicole gripped her hand.

"Don't take me back so soon," she pleaded.

Her voice was so supplicating that in a flash Josée understood what her daily life must be: this lonely vigil, this fear of death, this secret. She was overcome by pity. They went into a movie, but ten minutes later Nicole staggered to her feet, with Josée trailing after. The washroom was dismal. She supported Nicole with one hand and held the other to her damp forehead, feeling horrified and half-sick herself. When she got back to her own apartment and told Jacques the story of her day, he actually sympathized with her. "Poor old girl," he said, and for once he laid aside his medical books and suggested that they go out together.

Chapter 6

OR two days Josée tried to reach Bernard by telephone and tell him to come home. She made an attempt to send Nicole to Poitiers, but Nicole would not go. She was suffering constant pain, and this increased Josée's alarm. Finally Josée decided to go for Bernard in her car and asked Jacques to go with her. But he said that his classes would not allow him.

"It's only a day's trip, both ways," she insisted.

"Exactly. It's not too far for you to go alone."

Josée would have liked to beat him. He was so very sure of himself, so inclined to oversimplification that she would have given anything to see him, just for a moment, upset and on the defensive. Now he took her authoritatively by the shoulders.

"You're a first-rate driver and you like being by yourself. Besides, it's better that you should talk to this fellow alone. His relations with his wife aren't my affair. Only his relations with you concern me."

As he said this last sentence he batted his eyelids.

"Oh," she said, "it's been a long time, you know, since . . . "

"I don't know anything," he said. "If I did, I'd get out, that's all."

She looked at him with amazement and a feeling of something like hope.

"You mean you'd be jealous?"

"That's not the question. I wouldn't go halves."

He pulled her brusquely toward him and kissed her cheek. The awkwardness of his gesture caused Josée to throw her arms around his neck and press him to her. She kissed his neck and the shoulder of his heavy sweater, smiling to herself and repeating, pensively, "You'd get out, would you?" He did not move or say a word, and she felt as if she were in love with a bear she had met in a forest, a bear that loved her, in his own fashion, but was condemned to silence and could not tell his love.

"All right, all right," he grumbled.

She set out alone, then, very early in the morning, and drove slowly through the bare countryside. It was very cold, and a pale, gleaming sun shone down on the close-cropped fields. She had lowered the top of her car and rolled up the neck of the heavy sweater she had borrowed from Jacques, leaving her face exposed to the wind. At eleven o'clock she stopped near a side road leading through the fields, pulled the gloves off her icy hands, and lit the first cigarette she had smoked along the way. Sitting with her head thrown back against the seat and her eyes closed, she inhaled deeply. In spite of the cold she could feel the sun beat down on her eyelids. Everywhere there was silence. When she opened her eyes she saw a crow swooping down on the nearest field.

She got out of the car and started to walk down the road. She walked just as she did in Paris, with a nonchalant yet restless gait. She went by a farmhouse and a clump of trees; the road continued, as far as the eye could see, across the flat land. Soon she turned around and saw her faithful black car still waiting for her. She walked slowly back to the highway, with a satisfied feeling inside. "There must be an answer," she said out loud, "and even if there isn't . . . " The crow flew, cawing, away. "I like these intervals, these truces," she said, throwing her cigarette butt on the ground and carefully crushing it with her foot.

✿   ✿   ✿

She reached Poitiers toward six o'clock.

It took her some time to find Bernard's hotel, L'Ecu de France. The entrance hall had a dark, pretentious, and depressing air. She was led to Bernard's room through a long corridor with a corded tan carpet that caught her feet.

Bernard was sitting over his writing, with his back to the door, and said no more than a distracted "Come in." Surprised by the ensuing silence, he turned around. Only then did Josée think of his letter and of what her sudden arrival must signify to him. She drew back. But already Bernard was saying: "You're here!" and holding out his hands, while his face underwent a change so complete that Josée thought vaguely to herself: "So that's the face of a happy man." He pulled her to him and ran his hand with agonizing slowness through her hair, and she stood there, petrified, with only one thought: "I've got to set this straight; this is too hateful, I simply *must* tell him." But he had begun to talk, and every one of his words was a new obstacle to the truth.

"I never hoped. I shouldn't have dared . . . It's too wonderful. . . . How did I get along here without you? It's strange, this happiness . . . "

"Bernard," said Josée, "Bernard . . . "

"It's funny, you know; such a thing isn't ever the way one imagines it. I should have thought it would be a violent shock, that I'd bombard you with questions. And instead, it's as if I'd rediscovered something I'd known all along! Something that was missing . . . "

"Bernard, I must tell you . . . "

But she knew perfectly well that he was going to interrupt her, and that she would not speak.

"Don't tell me. This is the first real thing that has happened to me for so long . . . "

"That's probably true," Josée thought to herself. "There's a woman who loves him, and is in danger. He's on the brink of a real drama, and yet the only thing that has reality for him is this error he's making—that I'm letting him make. The happiness is real, and the love is not." And if she did not speak, it was because what she felt toward him was neither pity nor irony, but an immense complicity. One day she, too, would make the same mistake, and play at happiness with someone who didn't really love her.

He took her for a drink of white wine and *cassis* at the Café du Commerce, and talked eloquently to her about himself and her. It was a long time since she had heard talk of this kind, and she fell into a mood of tenderness and fatigue. Poitiers had closed in around her: the yellow and gray tints of the square, the dark figures of the occasional passers-by, the curious stares of the habitués of the café, and the bare branches of the plane trees. All these belonged to an absurd world which she had always known and must, at least once more, rediscover.

That night, lying next to the sleeping Bernard, with his long body which left her fundamentally indifferent, and a cumbersomely possessive arm thrown across her shoulders, she stared for a long time at the play of the automobile headlights over the flowers on the wallpaper. Her conscience was at rest. In two more days she would tell Bernard to go home. Three days out of her own life she would give him, three happy days. And doubtless these days would cost both of them dear. She thought how many nights Bernard must have lain awake, looking at the flashing headlights and the ugly flowers on the wall. She could afford to relieve him, even at the price of a merciful deception.

Chapter 7

ANDRÉ JOLYET had decided to make Béatrice his mistress. He found in her an interesting mixture of talent, on the one hand, and on the other the cruel sort of obtuseness that goes with ambition. Moreover, he appreciated her beauty, and the idea that they would make a handsome couple satisfied his ever-alert aesthetic sensibility. At fifty years of age he was excessively thin, with a somewhat unpleasantly sarcastic expression, and given to making the inappropriate gestures of a much younger man. Because refined tastes can lead to all sorts of aberrations, he had won, more than half mistakenly, the reputation of being a homosexual. He was one of those men commonly termed "picturesque," on account of the semi-independent, semi-insolent attitude which they assume in artistic circles. He would have been quite intolerable had it not been for the ironical fashion with which he regarded himself, and his genuine generosity.

To conquer Béatrice through her ambition would have been very easy. Jolyet was too well acquainted with such tacit bargains to find them amusing. He decided to penetrate one of her interior dramas and play in it a role which he imagined similar to that of Mosca—but a victorious Mosca—in *The Charterhouse of Parma*. Of course he had not the stature of Mosca any more than Béatrice had that of Sanseverina, although young Edouard Maligrasse did to some extent measure up to Fabrice in charm. But what did that matter? He moved among mediocre subjects, and in the happy mediocrity of his life he rarely found a case of genuine despair.

And so Béatrice was caught between power and love, or rather between two copybook pictures of them. On the one side there was the ironical, compromising, spectacular Jolyet, and on the other the tender, handsome, and romantic Edouard. She was in seventh heaven. The agony of having to make a choice made life very exciting, although, for strictly professional reasons, she knew quite well that Jolyet would be the winner. This made her bestow upon Edouard an affection which he would never have enjoyed had he been her undisputed master, and demonstrated that life is prone to giving with one hand what it takes away with the other.

Jolyet had allotted Béatrice the main part in his next play, without any condition whatsoever. He made no mention of his ultimate aims, and even complimented her upon Edouard's natural charm. He did give her to understand, however, that if she ever wearied of being squired by the younger man, he himself would be happy to escort her. This seemed like mere conventional courtesy, but it was really a great deal more, for he knew that women like Béatrice never leave one man unless it is for the sake of another. Meanwhile, Béatrice ceased enjoying her ambivalent role and took to worrying about the imprecise nature of Jolyet's courtship. In comparison with Jolyet's tantalizing indifference there was something dull about Edouard's devotion. She liked to conquer.

One evening Jolyet took her to dinner at Bougival. The weather was unseasonably warm and they went for a walk along the river. She had told Edouard that she was dining with her mother, a puritanical lady who did not approve of her escapades. The necessity of this lie, which ordinarily she would have told without effort, for some reason annoyed her. "I don't need to account to anyone for my time," she thought while she was telling it. As a matter of fact, Edouard did not demand any accounts from her. He asked only to be happy, and suffered no more than real disappointment over the loss of her company. But she insisted upon imagining that he was beside himself with jealousy and suspicion, and failed utterly to understand that his was the boundlessly confident love of a very young man.

Jolyet held her arm as they walked, listening distractedly to her exclamations over the coal barges. Whereas with Edouard she fell into the part of a devastating but rather world-weary woman, with Jolyet she could not help acting like an overenthusiastic child.

"How utterly charming!" she observed. "No one has really done justice to the beauty of the Seine and its barges. Except perhaps Verlaine . . . "

"Yes, perhaps so . . . "

Jolyet was delighted at the prospect of a long, poetic effusion. "Who knows if it's not because she makes me laugh that I'm pursuing her?" he thought smugly to himself.

"When I was young," Béatrice went on, waiting for a laugh, which he promptly supplied, "I mean, when I was little, I used to walk along the river this same way, telling myself that life held the most wonderful things in store. I was full of enthusiasm. And do you believe it? I still am."

"I do believe it," said Jolyet contentedly.

"And yet, nowadays, who cares about the river barges, or has any enthusiasm? Neither our books, nor our films, nor our stage."

Jolyet nodded his head, without making reply.

"I remember when I was ten years old," Béatrice said dreamily. "But why should you care about what I thought when I was a child?"

The brusqueness of her attack took Jolyet by surprise, and he suffered a moment of panic.

"Tell me about *your* childhood," said Béatrice. "I know so very little about you. You're really quite a riddle, you know . . ."

Jolyet searched desperately for some episode of his childhood, but memory failed him.

"I didn't have any childhood," he said with a stricken air.

"You *do* say the most horrifying things," said Béatrice, squeezing his arm.

Jolyet's childhood stopped there. But hers proceeded to adorn itself with stories of the most varied kinds, all of which pointed up the ingenuousness, timidity, and charm of Béatrice-as-a-child. She grew increasingly sentimental, and soon her hand and his met in his pocket.

"Your hand is cool," he said calmly.

Béatrice did not answer, but swayed toward him. Jolyet realized that she was ripe for the picking, and for a moment he wondered whether he really desired her. On the way back to Paris she leaned her head on his shoulder and her body against his. "It's in the bag," Jolyet thought to himself, a little wearily, and took her to her house, where he wanted to spend their first night together, since like many jaded men he liked his amorous adventures to offer him a change of scene. But at the front door Béatrice's silence and immobility made him aware that she was fast asleep. Very gently he woke her up, kissed her hand, and before she had fully come to, he put her in the elevator.

In front of the dying fire, Béatrice found Edouard. He was asleep, with his slender, tanned neck emerging from his opened shirt collar, and for a moment tears filled her eyes. She was vexed because she still didn't know whether Jolyet cared for her, and because, although she found Edouard so very handsome, she had no real use for him except as a companion for dining out. She woke him up. In warm, disjointed phrases torn from his sleep, he told her that he loved her, but in this she found no consolation, and under pretext of a headache she sent him home.

Meanwhile Jolyet, having left his car in the garage, walked gaily toward his own house, followed a woman, and finally went into a bar where he found Alain Maligrasse, who for the first time in all the twenty years of their acquaintance was dead drunk.

* * *

After his famous evening with Béatrice, Alain had decided never to see her again, since it was inconceivable that he should love anyone so stupid and so alien to him. Work, he felt sure, was his only salvation, and Bernard's absence from the office provided him with plenty of it. With Fanny's tacit support he tried to put Béatrice out of his mind, but of course quite unsuccessfully. He knew too well that passion is the salt of life, and that at the times when we are under its spell this salt is indispensable to us, even if we have got along very well without it before. In any case, he avoided seeing Béatrice and contented himself with asking Edouard to his house as often as possible and drinking in the signs of happiness—some of them purely imaginary—which he bore upon him. Thus, the trace of a razor cut on Edouard's neck could only be the mark of Béatrice's teeth, and his nephew's dark-circled eyes and weary air caused him acute pain. For, in spite of Bernard's involuntary laugh at the suggestion, Alain insisted upon considering her a very sensual woman. In the office he spent hours leafing through manuscripts and writing out notes on index cards about them. With a ruler in one hand and a pen dipped in green ink in the other, he would stop in the middle of underlining a title, the green line jumping the track and ruining the card, his heart pounding, just because something Béatrice had said to him in the restaurant had come suddenly to mind. Then he would throw the card in the wastebasket and begin over again. On the street he bumped into passers-by and failed to recognize his friends, thus living up more and more to the role of the charming but distracted middle-aged intellectual, which was exactly what was expected of him.

Every morning he opened the newspaper at the theatrical page, hoping to see one of the increasingly frequent mentions of Béatrice's name; then he let his eye run down the column of advertisements until he found it, in small letters, under the listing of the Théâtre de l'Ambigue. Immediately, he looked up, as if he had been caught doing something wrong, and then applied himself to scanning some other column. The day before he ran into Jolyet he had read the announcement, "No Tuesday performance," and his heart had stood still. He had known that any night, if necessity really impelled him, he could look at Béatrice, for ten minutes, on the stage. He had never actually gone to the theater at this time, but the idea that for one evening she would not even be there, available for him to see if he wanted, was more than he could stand. Béatrice, the beautiful and passionate. . . . He hid his face in his hands. This was the last straw. When he reached home he found Edouard there and learned that Béatrice was dining with her mother. But this piece of news did not console him; the harm was done and he had already discovered the depth of his wound. Pleading a dinner engagement, he fled from home and went to hang miserably about the Café de Flore, where he met two friends who gave him no help whatsoever. Seeing him so very pale, they urged him to drink first one and then two glasses of whisky. These were quite enough to upset his middle-aged liver, but he went on drinking, and at midnight he found himself standing elbow to elbow with Jolyet in a dubious little bar near the Madeleine.

❖　　❖　　❖

There could be little doubt that Alain was in a bad way, and besides, he had never been able to hold his liquor. His eyelids were swollen and his pale, delicate face was twitching distressingly. After their first effusive handshake, Jolyet succumbed to a moment of surprise. He would never have imagined finding Alain Maligrasse, alone and drunk, in a prostitutes' hangout. Then, remembering that curiosity is

78

the beginning of wisdom, he decided to find out what it was all about. He was fond of Alain, and so his curiosity was not altogether malevolent; it was friendly as well. And his interest was sharpened by the mingled nature of the feelings that prompted it.

Béatrice's name soon entered, quite naturally, into their conversation.

"I believe you've engaged her for your next show," said Alain.

He was in a good mood. Exhausted and happy, with the bar whirling around him. He was in that stage of love—and of liquor—where one is completely taken up with oneself, and can get along very well without the other party.

"I've just had dinner with her," said Jolyet.

"So she lies!" thought Alain, recalling what Edouard had told him.

He was glad, because this lie signified that she did not care very deeply for Edouard, but at the same time he was disappointed. If Béatrice could lie, then she was even more out of his grasp than he had imagined. Only real delicacy of feeling could have prompted her to care for him. And it appeared that in this she was lacking. On the whole, however, his reaction was one of relief.

"She's a good girl," he said. "Utterly charming."

"Beautiful!" said Jolyet, with a low laugh.

"Beautiful and passionate," said Alain, falling into his stock phrase for her, and saying it in such a tone of voice that Jolyet shot him a keen glance. There was a moment of silence and mutual scrutiny, during which each of them realized how little, in spite of their backslapping, he really knew about the other.

"I have a weakness for her," said Alain in a manner which he mistakenly imagined was casual.

"Nobody can blame you for that," Jolyet answered.

He was tempted to laugh, but at the same time he wanted to console him. His immediate reaction had been: "Surely it could be arranged," but a second later he realized that this was not true. Béatrice would more readily give herself to a one-eyed old man. In love, as in finance, only the rich can get credit, and Alain was self-consciously poor. Jolyet ordered two more scotches. He looked forward to making a night of it. These were the things he enjoyed: an unexpected face, the feel of a glass in his hand, low-voiced confidences that went on until dawn and were succeeded by exhaustion.

"At my age, what can I do?" Alain asked.

Jolyet winced before answering: "Everything!" For Alain's age was also his own.

"She's not meant for me, that's all," said Alain.

"No one's 'meant' for another," said Jolyet at random.

"Yes, Fanny was meant for me. But now, this obsession. . . . You can't imagine how terrible it is. I feel gouty and ridiculous. And yet it's the only thing that's alive. All the rest . . ."

" 'All the rest is literature,' " Jolyet supplied, laughing. "I understand. But your real trouble is that Béatrice has no brains. She's ambitious, though, and today even that's something. So many people are nothing at all."

"I do have something to give her," mused Alain. "Confidence, respect, a certain amount of refinement. Oh, and then! . . . "

Before Jolyet's gaze he stopped short and vaguely waved his hand, spilling some of the whisky onto the floor. He apologized to the proprietress of the bar, and Jolyet felt an immense pity for him.

"Try your luck, old man," he said; "tell her your story. She can't do anything worse than say no, and in that case you'll know where you stand."

"Try my luck now, when she's in love with my nephew? That would be writing off my only chance, if I have one."

"No, that's where you're all wrong. There are cases, of course, where the timing is important. But Béatrice isn't one of them. She picks the moment for her own seduction."

Alain ran a hand through his hair, and because there was so little of it, it was a miserable gesture. Jolyet tried vaguely to think up a stealthy way of giving Béatrice to dear old Maligrasse on a silver platter—after he was through with her himself, of course. Failing to find a solution, he ordered another round of drinks. Meanwhile, Alain was orating about love, and one of the girls standing at the bar was nodding her approval. Jolyet knew her well, and before going away he recommended Alain to her attentions. A pale, damp dawn hung over the Champs-Elysées, and before lighting a cigarette he breathed deeply of the early-morning country air of Paris. "A most entertaining evening," he murmured with a smile, and set out at a brisk, youthful pace for his own dwelling.

Chapter 8

"**I**'LL call you up tomorrow," said Bernard, putting his head through the car window.

Probably, as is often the case with a great passion, the moment of separation brought him a kind of relief. Now at last there was time to be happy. Josée smiled. She was rediscovering Paris at night, the hum of the traffic, and a life of her own.

"Hurry up," she said.

After watching him go in the door of his apartment house, she drove away. The day before she had told Bernard that Nicole was in danger and he must go home. She had expected some sort of violent reaction, either surprise or fear, but all he said was:

"Is that why you came?"

"No," she had told him, and she herself no longer knew how much cowardice there was in this reply. Perhaps she had wished, as much as he, to protect the strange sweetness of those three gray days in Poitiers: the slow walks through the frozen fields, the long, soberly worded conversations, the tenderness of the nights, all built upon the common denominator of their misunderstanding, which gave a paradoxical honesty to the affair.

She got back to her own apartment toward eight o'clock and hesitated a moment before questioning the maid about Jacques. The maid told her that he had gone away two days after her, leaving a pair of shoes behind him. She telephoned to the house where he had a room, but was told that he had left it and given no forwarding address. She hung up the receiver, watching the light fall on the rug of her overly large living room, and feeling lost and tired. Looking at herself in the mirror, she saw that she was twenty-five years old, with three wrinkles and an over-powering wish to see Jacques. Somehow, she had hoped to find him there, in his duffle coat, and to explain that her absence was totally unimportant. She telephoned Fanny and was promptly asked to dinner.

Fanny looked thin and Alain behaved as if his thoughts were far away. Josée found the dinner unbearably painful, in spite or perhaps because of Fanny's desperate efforts to give it a conventional air. As soon as they had had their coffee, Alain asked to be excused and went off to bed. For a few minutes Fanny withstood Josée's questioning eyes;

then she got up, looking very tiny, and started to put something on the mantelpiece in order.

"Alain had too much to drink last night; you'll have to forgive him," she said at last.

"Too much to drink? Alain?"

It was so unlike Alain Maligrasse, so incredible that Josée couldn't help laughing.

"Don't laugh," Fanny said brusquely.

"I'm sorry."

Then Fanny told her that what had seemed like no more than a passing fancy on the part of Alain was ruining both their lives. Josée tried in vain to assure her that it would probably quickly pass away.

"He can't love Béatrice for long. She's quite impossible. Oh, I'll grant you she has charm, but she has no real feelings, and he won't go on loving all alone. How far has she . . . ?"

She didn't dare complete the question. She couldn't imagine anyone going very far with a man as polite as Alain.

"No, no," said Fanny angrily. "I'm sorry I even mentioned it. I felt so alone . . . "

At midnight Josée went away. She had been afraid all evening that the sound of their voices might bring Alain out of his room to join them. Unhappiness frightened her, and she saw no way to combat a hopeless passion. As she left the house she was overcome by the messiness of the whole situation.

She must find Jacques, even if he were to beat her, or

push her away. Anything was better than these complications. And she made her way to the Latin Quarter.

*   *   *

The night was dark and there was a light rain. It was horrible to be wandering about Paris, torn between fatigue and the necessity of finding Jacques. He must be in one of the cafés along the boulevard Saint-Michel, or with a friend . . . perhaps even with a girl. She no longer knew this part of the city, and the cellar where she had danced in her student days was now a tourist mecca. Suddenly she realized how little she knew about Jacques' life. She had thought of it as that of the typical, rather brutish student that he appeared to be. Now she searched her memory feverishly for some name or address which he might have casually dropped in her presence. She went into the cafés and looked around, while the young men's whistles and interjections fell like so many blows about her head. For a long time she had lived through no such miserable anxiety. And her sense of the probable futility of her search, above all the thought of Jacques' closed, hostile face, only served to increase her despair.

In the tenth café she saw him. He was standing with his back to her, over the pin-ball machine. She recognized him immediately by the shape of his back and his straight neck, overgrown with coarse, reddish-blond hair. For a moment the thought struck her that this unbarbered look was like

Bernard's, that it must be the sign of a deserted and lonely man. She could not make up her mind to step forward, and stood her ground, while her heart missed a beat.

"Do you want to order a drink?"

The owner of the café precipitated the climax. Josée moved forward. She realized that her coat was too well cut for a place of this caliber, and mechanically pulled up the collar as she stopped behind Jacques' back and called his name. He did not look around, but she could see a deep flush rise from his neck to the edge of his cheek.

"Have you something to say to me?" he asked.

They sat down, without his even looking at her. He asked her what she would have to drink and then lowered his eyes, with an air of finality, to his square hands.

"You must try to understand," Josée told him. And she embarked wearily upon her story, with the feeling that all these things, Poitiers, Bernard, and the headlights on the wall, were completely remote and unreal. She was across a table from Jacques, and he was supremely alive. There he sat before her, like a solid block, inaccessible to mere words, holding her fate in his hands. She waited, and anything she said was simply a means of making the unbearable moments of waiting go by.

"I don't like someone to make a fool of me," he said at last.

"That's not it . . ." Josée began.

He looked at her out of furious gray eyes.

"That *is* it, exactly. When you're living with one fellow,

87

you don't go off and spend three days with another. Or at least you give due notice."

"I've tried to explain . . . "

"I don't give a damn for your explanation. I'm not a little boy; I'm a man. I went away, I even moved out of my own room . . ." And he added, with rising anger: "There aren't many girls who have pushed me that far. How did you find me?"

"For the last hour I've been looking for you in all the cafés."

She closed her eyes in utter exhaustion, feeling the weight of the dark circles around them. There was a moment of silence, and then he asked in a choked voice:

"Why?"

She stared at him uncomprehendingly.

"Why were you looking for me?"

She had closed her eyes again and thrown back her head. A vein in her throat was throbbing, and she heard herself say:

"I needed you, that's why."

And the realization that this was at last true made her eyes fill with tears.

Later they went home together. And when he took her into his arms she rediscovered the meaning of a body and the motions and pleasure of love. She kissed his hand and fell asleep, with her lips on the palm. For some time he remained awake. Then he carefully pulled the sheet over her shoulders before turning onto his other side.

Chapter 9

AT HIS apartment door Bernard found two nurses, one about to relieve the other. He was shocked into awareness of a disaster and at the same time of his own incapacity to be moved by it. He was cold with fear. The nurses told him that Nicole had had a miscarriage two days before, and that although she was out of danger, Dr. Marin was taking no chances and had prescribed twenty-four-hour nursing care. The two women were staring at him, sitting in judgment upon him, and no doubt expecting him to furnish some reason for not having been there. But he pushed them aside without saying a word and went into the bedroom.

Nicole lay with her head turned toward the door. The atrocious porcelain lamp which he had never dared to criticize because it had been given to her by her mother shed a dim light over the room. She was very pale and her face did not flicker when she saw him. She had the obtuse, dignified expression of an animal in pain.

"Nicole."

He sat down on the bed and took her hand. She looked quietly at him, then suddenly her eyes filled with tears. He drew her cautiously into his arms and she let her head drop onto his shoulder. "What can I do or say?" Bernard wondered. "And what a stinker I am!" He ran his hand over her head, catching his fingers in her long hair and mechanically disentangling it. She was still feverish. "I've got to say something," thought Bernard. "I've got to find something to say."

"Bernard," she began, "our child . . ."

She sobbed brokenly, and he felt her shoulders heaving against him. "There, there," he said soothingly. Suddenly he realized that this was his wife, his possession, and his alone, that she had no thought but for him, that she had come close to dying. He realized that she was doubtless the only thing he really did possess, and one that he had very nearly lost forever. Possession and pity—pity for the two of them—suddenly tore him apart, and he turned his head away brusquely. "We are born crying, and for good reason," he reflected. "And the rest of our lives is bound to be a muted reiteration of that cry." The feeling that rose up in his throat and drained his strength away, casting him, in his turn, upon the shoulder of this woman he no longer loved, was assuredly an echo of the cry with

90

which he had been born. Everything in between was no more than a sporadic tremor, an attempt to escape, a bit of play-acting. For a moment he forgot all about Josée and gave himself up to his despair.

*　　*　　*

Later on he consoled Nicole as best he could. He spoke, with satisfaction, about his book, and talked tenderly about their future and the children that would one day be theirs. Through her tears she said she had chosen the name of Christopher for this lost baby, and he approved but put in a word for "Anne." That made her smile, because it is a known fact that every man's heart is set on having a daughter. Meanwhile, Bernard began to wonder how he was going to make a telephone call to Josée. He leaped at the excuse of going to buy some cigarettes. On his way he blessed the manifold uses of the tobacconist. The cashier greeted him with a joyful "So you're home again?" and he drank a glass of cognac at the bar before asking for the telephone slug. He was going to say to Josée: "I need you." It was perfectly true, and yet it didn't make any difference. Whenever he had spoken of love, she had spoken of love's brief duration. "A year, or even two months from now, you won't love me any more." Josée was the only person he knew who had a real consciousness of time. Everyone else, including himself, was driven by some very fundamental instinct to try, or pretend, to believe that love could last and solitude be dispelled forever.

But when he made the call, there was no answer. Thinking back to the night when he had telephoned and that vile young man had picked up the receiver, he smiled with relief. Josée must be sleeping like a log, with her hand lying outstretched and open at her side: this was the only one of her gestures to indicate any need for another person.

* * *

Edouard Maligrasse was serving the herb tea which, for the last week, Béatrice had taken to drinking. He handed one cup to her and another to Jolyet, who at once laughed and declared that it was poison. The two men proceeded to pour themselves scotches; Béatrice called them a pair of alcoholics, and Edouard leaned happily back in his chair. He had gone to call for her at the theater and she had asked Jolyet to come have a nightcap in her apartment. It was raining outside, and they toasted themselves beside the fire, while Jolyet told amusing stories.

Béatrice was very much put out with Edouard for acting as if he were the master of the house and serving the tea. Did he want to compromise her? No one is more conventional than a woman who is falling out of love. Béatrice had forgotten that Jolyet knew all about their affair, and also that, if Edouard made familiar gestures of this kind, it was because she had treated him like a page boy. She turned now to Jolyet and talked about his projected play, refusing to let Edouard have any share in the conversation. It was Jolyet who finally insisted upon paying attention to him.

"How's the insurance business?" he asked.

"Very good," answered Edouard, blushing. He owed a hundred thousand francs, or two months' salary, to his supervisor, and fifty thousand francs to Josée. He tried not to think about these debts, but all day long they weighed upon his mind.

"I wish I were in some such line," said Jolyet, quite heedlessly. "Then I shouldn't have to kill myself with worry to raise the money for a play."

"I can't see you in that 'line,' as you call it," said Béatrice, with a vindictive little laugh aimed at Edouard. "Why, it's almost like selling door to door!"

Edouard did not move, but looked at her with amazement, while Jolyet rushed into the breach.

"You're quite wrong there," he insisted. "I'd make a very good insurance salesman. All my powers of persuasion would be called into play. 'Madame, you're very pale; I think you may be going to die. Take out an insurance policy, so your husband can have a nest egg for his next marriage!'"

And he laughed at his own joke. Edouard put in a feeble protest.

"I don't work at the selling end, really. I have an office job." And then, fearful lest he had made himself seem too important, he added: "It's terribly tedious, of course. I file . . ."

"Will you have some more scotch, André?" Béatrice interrupted.

There was an embarrassed silence, which Jolyet broke by another heroic effort.

"No, thanks. By the way, there was a first-rate film some time ago called *Death Insurance*. Did you ever see it?"

The question was addressed to Edouard. But Béatrice could not contain herself. She wanted Edouard to go, but it was obvious that he meant to stay. For three months now she had made him feel as if this were the natural thing to do. Now he meant to stay and sleep in her bed, and the prospect was boring. So she answered on his behalf:

"You know, Edouard's a country boy."

"I saw it at Caen," Edouard put in.

"Quite the big city, eh?" said Béatrice with a mocking air.

Edouard got up, feeling dizzy. He looked so taken aback that Jolyet swore he would repay Béatrice in the same coin someday. Once he was on his feet, Edouard hesitated. He couldn't believe that Béatrice no longer loved him, or even that he had in some way annoyed her. To harbor such thoughts would have been to bring the whole fabric of his present life down around his shoulders, and he was totally unprepared for such a collapse. However, he did manage to say:

"Am I being a bother?"

"Not at all!" Béatrice answered savagely.

Edouard sat down. In the warmth of the bed, he would

ask Béatrice what was the matter. Under the cover of darkness, her upturned, tragic face and surrendered body would give him a reply. He loved Béatrice physically, in spite of her detachment. Indeed her very coldness and immobility inspired his most considerate, most passionate gestures. Then, like a youth in love with a corpse, he would lie propped up on one elbow, watching her sleep.

That night she was more distant than ever. Béatrice was a stranger to remorse; that was part of her charm. Edouard slept badly and began to believe that he was going to be unhappy.

* * *

Because she was not at all sure of Jolyet, Béatrice did not wish to get rid of Edouard altogether. No one had ever loved her so unreservedly, and such devotion was not to be thrown away. Nevertheless she spaced their meetings, and more and more frequently Edouard found himself delivered up, alone, to the city.

Edouard's Paris was made up of two itineraries: one from his office to the theater and the other from the theater to Béatrice's apartment. Everyone has known these miniature villages which frame a big-city passion. At the beginning of Béatrice's defection, Edouard fancied himself definitely lost. Mechanically he followed the same streets as before. Since Béatrice had now forbidden him to come to her dressing room, he bought a ticket for every evening performance and listened distractedly until Béatrice appeared on the stage. She was playing the part of a lady's maid who came on during the second act and said to the young man who had arrived ahead of time to call for her mistress:

"You'll find out, Monsieur! For a woman, the exact time is often the right time. After the exact time may be the right time, too. But before the exact time is never the right time, never, never!"

For some unfathomable reason these insignificant sentences shattered Edouard's heart. He waited impatiently for the three bits of dialogue immediately preceding them, which he knew by memory, and when Béatrice actually spoke he closed his eyes. Their sound recalled the happy days when she had not had so many headaches and business engagements and lunches with her mother. He did not dare say to himself "the days when she loved me," for in spite of his ingenuousness he had always known that he was the lover and she was the object of love. From this fact he drew a bitter satisfaction which he hardly ventured to put into words: "At least she can't say that she doesn't love me *any more.*"

Soon, in spite of all the money he was saving on lunches, he could no longer afford even a folding seat in the aisle, and the meetings with Béatrice were further and further apart. Edouard said nothing, because he was afraid. Since he did not know how to bluff, his conversation was limited to a mutely passionate question which she found highly disturbing to her peace of mind. However, she was studying her part in Jolyet's production, and it was as though she hardly noticed Edouard's face any longer, or, for that matter, that of Jolyet, either. She had a role, a really big role, and her bedroom mirror was once more her best friend. It reflected not the outstretched body and bent neck of a young man with chestnut hair, but the figure of herself as the heroine of a nineteenth-century drama.

In order to stifle his nostalgic desire for Béatrice's body, Edouard took long walks from one end of the city to the other. He walked five or ten miles a day, and feminine passers-by, struck by his hollow cheeks and absent, haunted air, would have been glad to console him had he paid them the least bit of attention. Edouard was trying to understand, to find out what he could have done to lose Béatrice's favor. He couldn't know that his unpardonable sin was the fact that he was too deserving.

One evening, when he was in a state of acute distress and had not eaten for all of two days, he found himself in front of the Maligrasse door. Impulsively he rang the bell. His uncle was lying on a couch, reading a theatrical magazine instead of his usual *Nouvelle Revue Française*. They exchanged a look of mutual surprise, for both of them were battle-scarred, without imagining that it was for the same reason. Fanny came in, kissed Edouard, and expressed astonishment over his condition. She herself was looking younger and more agreeable than usual, having decided to ignore Alain's lovesickness, take beauty treatments, and make things as pleasant as possible for him at home. She knew perfectly well that this was a woman's magazine formula for living, but since intelligence seemed to play no part in the story, she did not hesitate. Once she had got over her initial resentment, her main purpose was to assure Alain's happiness, or at least his peace of mind.

"Dear Edouard, you look tired. Is it your work in the insurance office? You ought to take better care of yourself, you know."

"I'm hungry," Edouard admitted.

Fanny couldn't help laughing.

"Follow me to the kitchen," she said. "There are ham and cheese in the icebox, I know."

They were just about to leave the room when they were halted by Alain's deliberately colorless and singsong voice.

"Edouard, did you see the picture of Béatrice in this issue of *Opéra?*"

Edouard leaped to look over his uncle's shoulder. Underneath the picture of Béatrice in evening dress was the caption: "Young Béatrice B . . . is rehearsing the leading role in the new play at the Athénée." Fanny gazed for a second at the backs of Alain and Edouard, as they bent over the magazine close together. Then she turned on her heels and went out to the kitchen. There, looking into a small mirror, she said aloud to herself: "It gets on my nerves; yes, decidedly!"

A moment later Alain called to her: "I'm going out."

"Will you be back tonight?" Fanny asked, without raising her voice.

"I don't know."

He didn't look at her as he went out. He never looked at her any more. Recently he had been spending his nights drinking at the bar near the Madeleine with the girl he had met there, and ending up in her room. Usually he did not touch her, but simply listened quietly to the stories she had to tell about her clients. She had a furnished room near the Gare Saint-Lazare, and the light of the street lamp below filtered through the shutters and made stripes on the ceiling. When he had had a great deal to drink, he fell asleep right away. Because he did not know that Jolyet was giving the girl money on his behalf, he attributed her kindness to spontaneous affection, and as a matter of fact she did find his good breeding and gentle manners very agreeáble. He forbade himself to think of Fanny, whose good humor gave him a vague sense of reassurance.

Meanwhile, Fanny asked Edouard: "Has it been a long time since your last meal?"

She watched indulgently the way he gobbled his food, and the warmth of her look made him unspeakably grateful to her. Gradually he let himself go. He had been too unhappy, too alone, and Fanny was terribly kind. Quickly he gulped down some beer to loosen the tight feeling in his throat.

"Two days," he answered.

"No money?"

He nodded, and Fanny said indignantly:

"You're quite mad, Edouard. You know that you're always welcome here. Come whenever you want, before you get to the point of fainting away. It's perfectly ridiculous."

"*I'm* ridiculous, and I know it," said Edouard. "There's no other way to describe me."

The beer had gone to his head, and for the first time he thought of freeing himself from his enslaving passion. After all, there were other things in life: friendship, affection, and the understanding of someone like the remarkable Fanny, whom his uncle had had the wisdom and great good fortune to marry. They went back to the drawing room, and Fanny picked up her knitting, that great resource of unhappy women. They lit a fire and Edouard sat down at the foot of the chaise longue. Soon both of them felt better.

"Tell me what's wrong," Fanny said after a moment.

She knew that he was going to talk about Béatrice, but she was not altogether sorry to have this occasion to hear something about her. She had always found Béatrice beautiful, lively, and rather stupid. Perhaps Edouard could explain the secret of her charm. Although she realized that Alain was pursuing an idea rather than a flesh-and-blood woman.

"You know, of course, that we . . . that Béatrice and I . . ."

Edouard's tongue tripped on these words. Fanny shot him an almost conspiratorial smile and he blushed, with a

100

stab of regret in his heart. To all the people he had seen in this house he had seemed to be Béatrice's happy lover. Now he was anything but happy. In a jerky style, he began his story. As he tried to explain, as much to himself as to his hearer, the causes of his woe, it stood out more and more clearly in his eyes, and at the end he put his head on Fanny's knees and let himself be carried away by a sort of relieving spasm. Fanny ran her hand over his hair and murmured an occasional "Poor boy!" in a tone of infinite compassion. She was almost sorry when he raised his head, for his hair was pleasing to the touch.

"Forgive me," said Edouard shamefacedly. "I've had no one to talk to for so long."

"I know exactly how it is," said Fanny, without thinking.

"But there's Alain . . ." Edouard protested.

Then he stopped short, mindful of Alain's odd behavior a short time before and the way he had walked out of the house. Fanny thought that of course he knew, and began to talk freely of her husband's folly. Only the look of utter astonishment on Edouard's face revealed that he did not know. Alain would have found the astonishment most unflattering, and yet it was natural enough that the idea of his uncle's pining for Béatrice should leave Edouard completely dumbfounded. Then, analyzing the implications of this state of affairs, he felt a sudden sympathy for Fanny and seized her hand. He was sitting by her knees on the chaise longue, and in a moment of emotional exhaustion he leaned his head wearily against her shoulder. Fanny laid down her knitting. He dozed a little. She put out the light, so that his sleep might be unbroken. After that she did not stir; her chest barely rose and fell, while she felt his breath on her neck. She was troubled by his nearness and tried not to think.

An hour later, Edouard woke up, and his first gesture was instinctively masculine. It was dark; he lay on a woman's shoulder. Fanny held him to her, and one gesture followed another. Edouard did not wake up again until dawn. He was in a strange bed, and above the sheet, on a level with his eyes, there lay a slightly wrinkled, heavily ringed hand. He closed his eyes for a moment, then got up and went away, while Fanny pretended to be sleeping.

*   *   *

Josée called Bernard up the next day and said she must talk to him. Bernard understood. From the calm way in which he took this announcement he realized that he had understood from the start. He loved and needed her, but she did not love him. The corollary to these three propositions was a long train of weakness and suffering, from which it would take him some time to escape. The last days at Poitiers were the only windfall he could expect from the present year. Then, because he was happy, he had lived like a man. For unhappiness has nothing to teach, and resignation is ugly.

It was pouring rain, and people said this was no sort of spring. Bernard walked to his last meeting with Josée, and from far away he saw her waiting for him. Everything took place as if in a drama that he had seen played long before.

❋   ❋   ❋

They sat on a bench, under the rain, both of them dead tired. She said she didn't love him, and he said it didn't matter, and the poverty of their words brought tears to their eyes. The bench where they sat overlooked the ceaseless traffic of the Place de la Concorde, and the city lights were as cruel as memories of childhood. They held hands, and his teary face bent over the rain-splashed face of Josée. The kisses they exchanged were those of passionate lovers, for fate had botched both their lives, and they didn't even care. Yet, they were truly fond of each other. The soggy cigarette that Bernard tried vainly to light was a symbol of all they had in common, for they could never be really happy, and they knew it. And at the same time they knew, obscurely, that it didn't matter. It simply didn't matter.

❋   ❋   ❋

A week after the evening he had spent at the Maligrasses', Edouard found a legal summons demanding that he pay the money he owed to his tailor. He had spent his last few francs on a great bunch of flowers for Fanny, which had, without his knowing it, touched her almost to the point of tears. Now there was only one person to whom he could turn, as he had turned once before, and that was Josée. He went to see her on Saturday morning, but only Jacques was there, deep in his medical studies. He told Edouard that Josée would be home for lunch and went back to his books. Edouard paced up and down the room, feeling very uncomfortable over the necessity of waiting for Josée's return. He began to lose his nerve and to cudgel his brain for some pretext other than the true one for his intrusion. Jacques looked up at him and held out a cigarette. The silence was unbearable.

"You don't look very happy," Jacques said at last.

Edouard shrugged his shoulders apologetically and Jacques continued to look at him with a sympathetic eye.

"It's none of my business, of course," he said, "but I've seldom seen anyone look as if he were in so much of a jam."

It seemed as if he were about to whistle with reluctant admiration, and Edouard smiled. Jacques was a good fellow. He wasn't like Jolyet or the hangers-on at the theater. All at once, Edouard felt once more like a man.

"Women," he said briefly.

"Tough luck!" said Jacques.

There was a long silence, while both of them explored their memories. Then Jacques coughed and said interrogatively:

"Josée?"

Edouard shook his head. He couldn't resist impressing the younger man.

"No, an actress."

"I don't know any actresses, myself," Jacques admitted. "But I can imagine that in their special way they may be hard to handle."

"They are, believe me."

"I'll see if I can't dig up something to drink," said Jacques.

He got up, giving Edouard a rough but friendly pat on the shoulder as he went by, and came back with a bottle of Bordeaux wine. By the time Josée arrived they were in excellent spirits and talking about women with a nonchalant and knowing air.

"Hello, Edouard. You look a bit under the weather."

Josée liked Edouard. He had an open way about him which she found extremely appealing.

"How is Béatrice?" she asked.

Jacques signaled to her wildly and was caught in the act by Edouard. All three of them looked at one another, and Josée burst out laughing.

"Apparently things aren't going well," she said. "Why don't you stay to lunch?"

In the afternoon they drove out to the country and went for a long walk in the woods, with Béatrice the chief subject of their conversation. Edouard and Josée strolled arm in arm along one path after another, while Jacques plunged into thickets, tossed pine cones into the air, and played at nature-boy, joining the others from time to time with a brief statement to the effect that this Béatrice deserved a good spanking. Josée laughed, and Edouard began to feel better. Finally he managed to blurt out that he needed money, and she told him not to worry.

"I really need friends, even more," Edouard blushingly added.

At this point Jacques made one of his sallies out of the underbrush and said to count on him for that. Josée seconded him enthusiastically. From then on the three of them spent their evenings together. In one another's company, they felt young, companionable, and almost happy.

But if Josée and Jacques to some extent cheered Edouard, they also depressed him. After hearing his account of the turn his relationship with Béatrice had taken, they gave as their opinion that it was all over. But Edouard was not entirely sure. He occasionally saw Béatrice, between rehearsals, when according to her mood she sometimes greeted him as "darling boy" and gave him a tender kiss, and at others looked right through him, with an irritated air. He resolved to settle the question one way or the other, to get it off his chest, if that was the right expression, without further delay.

He met Béatrice at a café across from the theater, and found her more beautiful than ever, pale and tired, and wearing that tragic and noble mask he loved so well. She was in one of her distracted moods, and this dampened his hopes of hearing her protest: "Why, of course I love you!" Nevertheless, he stuck to his plan.

"How's the play?" he asked.

"I shall be in rehearsal all summer."

Béatrice did not wish to linger. Jolyet was to drop in at the rehearsal. She still didn't know whether he loved or desired her, or whether she was simply an actress in his eyes.

"There is something I must tell you," Edouard was saying.

He bent his head and she saw the roots of his fine hair, which she had once taken so much pleasure in caressing. At present he meant nothing to her, one way or the other.

"I love you," he said, without looking up. "And I think you don't love me; perhaps you never did."

He was obsessed by the need of certitude. Was it possible that so many nights of sighs and laughter? . . . But she was looking over his head and did not reply.

"Tell me," he said at last.

She must speak. It simply couldn't go on this way. The agony was more than he could bear. His left hand grasped her right hand, and brought her reluctantly back to earth. "What a bore!" she was thinking. But she said:

"Edouard dear, one thing I must say. I don't love you any more, that's true. But I do care for you, and always will. And I *did* love you very much, you know."

As she said these words, she was aware of the importance of the phrase "very much" in sentimental affairs. Edouard raised his head.

"I don't believe you," he said sadly.

They looked each other in the eye, something they had

rarely done before. And she wanted to cry out: "No, I never did love you. What of it? Was there any reason why I should? Is loving necessary? Don't you think I have anything else on my mind?" She was thinking of the stage, with the play of footlights upon it, or suddenly darkened. A wave of happiness rolled over her.

"Don't believe me, if you don't want to," she said. "But no matter what happens, I'll always be your friend. You're a most engaging fellow."

"But my nights . . ." he interrupted in a low voice.

"What do you mean by 'your nights'? You can always . . ."

She stopped abruptly, because Edouard had gone. He was tramping through the streets like a wild man, murmuring "Béatrice, Béatrice," and wanting to knock his head against a wall. He hated her, he loved her, and the memory of their first night together caused him to stumble and nearly fall. After hours of aimless walking, he wound up at Josée's. She sat him down, gave him a tall glass of whisky, and said nothing. Soon he fell asleep. When he woke up, Jacques was there. They went out, all three of them, and came back half-seas over. Edouard was installed in the guest room and lived there until summer. He was still in love with Béatrice, and, like his uncle, opened every newspaper to the theatrical page.

*　　*　　*

Summer fell upon Paris, with everyone still intently following his own subterranean course of passion or habit and looking up like a startled creature of the night at the blazing June sun. Now, all of a sudden, there was an impelling necessity to go away, to give a continuation or a meaning to the winter that had just gone by. Everyone recovered the feeling of liberty and solitude that comes with the approach of a long vacation and wondered with whom, and under what circumstances, he would pass the time. Only Béatrice, who was forced by her rehearsals to stay in town, escaped, not without complaint, from this problem. Alain Maligrasse had taken seriously to drink, and Béatrice was by now no more than an excuse for his aberration. He had got into the habit of saying: "I have a job that I like, a charming wife, and a most agreeable existence. So what?" To this question no one was able to give him an answer. Only Jolyet pointed out to him that he was posing this paradox a little late in the game. But of course it wasn't too late to go in for heavy drinking.

So it was that Alain Maligrasse fell into a state of confusion, and sought remedies more commonly adopted by much younger men, namely, alcohol and women. That is the drawback of a precocious grand passion for such a thing as literature: it leaves you an easy prey to some pettier one, which is all the more dangerous because it is tardy. Alain gave himself up to his new vices with the comfortable sensation of having at last found a haven. His life was a series of restless nights, when his bar-friend, Jacqueline, delighted him by making jealous scenes, and of days spent in a coma. "I'm like Baudelaire's stranger," he told the flabbergasted Bernard. "I'm looking at the clouds, the marvelous clouds."

Bernard could have understood his loving Jacqueline, but he couldn't see how he put up with such a disrupted existence. With all of this, he was also vaguely envious, since he, too, would have liked to take to drink in order to put Josée out of his mind. Still, escape was not his principal aim. One afternoon he went to ask Fanny for a bit of information, and was amazed by the amount of weight she had lost, and her defensive air. It was quite natural that they should talk of Alain, for everyone knew how much too much he was drinking. Bernard had taken over his work in the office, but the astonishment there was still too great for the situation to have led to dismissal.

"What can I do?" Bernard asked Fanny.

"Nothing at all," was Fanny's tranquil answer. "There is a whole side of him which I knew nothing about . . . and probably neither did he, for that matter. I suppose that when two people live for twenty years together in such total ignorance . . ."

She made a little grimace of pain which wrung Bernard's heart. He reached out to take her hand and was surprised by the vivacity with which, blushing, she drew it away.

"It's just something Alain has to go through," he said. "It isn't serious, really . . ."

"Béatrice is the one that set him off. She made him feel that his life was empty. . . . Yes, yes, I know," she concluded wearily, "I'm the perfect wife . . ."

110

Bernard thought of the excited way in which Alain talked about every detail of his new life, the significance he attached to the sordid scenes of the bar near the Madeleine. He kissed Fanny's hand and went away.

On his way out Bernard met Edouard, who was coming to call on Fanny. They had never spoken of their night together, and she had done no more than thank him, quite unemotionally, for the flowers which he had sent her the following day. He would sit at her feet and they would look out through the open French window at Paris lying in the hot June sun. They talked in a tender, desultory manner about life and the country, and Fanny had more than ever a sensation of impending doom.

At her feet, Edouard was prey to a confused sense of sorrow and an uneasiness so strong that it brought him back every three or four days, in order to see with his own eyes that he had done her no harm. It was with a sensation of relief and something close to gaiety that he went from her house to Josée's apartment. There he found Jacques, in a state of wild concern over his recent examinations, and Josée surrounded by maps of Sweden, where the three of them meant to take an automobile trip at the end of the month.

*   *   *

The trip came off, as planned. Meanwhile the Maligrasses were invited for a month to the house of friends, in the country, where Alain spent most of his time with a

111

bottle. Béatrice managed to leave her rehearsals long enough to join her mother on the Riviera and add some new admirers to her train. Only Bernard stayed all summer in Paris, working at his novel, while Nicole went to visit her parents. All over the depopulated city the hot sidewalks rang to the sound of Bernard's feet. Here was the bench where he had given Josée a farewell kiss, there the café from which he had called her up that dreadful night and found she was not alone; on this very spot he had suddenly stood still, overcome by happiness, on the evening of their return from Poitiers, when he had thought he really had something at last. . . . After the sunlit streets, his office seemed dustier than ever; he read a great many books, and his obsession was punctuated by moments of extraordinary calm. He walked toward the shimmering bridges laden with regret and the memory of regret. Often a vision of Poitiers in the rain veiled the reality of Paris in the sun. Then, in September, everyone came back to town. He caught sight of Josée at the wheel of her car, and she drew up to the curb in order to speak to him. Leaning on the door to look at her slender, tanned face under its mass of black hair, he knew he was never going to get over it; no, never.

Yes, they had had a good trip, Sweden was very beautiful; Edouard had run the car into a ditch, but no harm was done, because Jacques . . . She stopped short, seeing the angry look on his face.

"You may think I'm vulgar," he said, "but I don't find this peaceful happiness becoming to you."

She did not answer, but gave him a sad smile.

"Forgive me," he said. "I'm in no position to speak of happiness, peaceful or otherwise. And I haven't forgotten that I owe you my only happiness of this year."

She laid her hand on his. Their hands had the same shape, except that Bernard's was larger. Both of them noticed it at the same time, without speaking. She drove away and he went home. He was able to be kind to Nicole and make her content, thanks to the calm which he had distilled from his sorrow. That was something, at least.

*   *   *

"Béatrice, there's your cue . . ."

Béatrice came out of the shadowy wings into the glare of the footlights and held out her arms. "No wonder she's so empty," Jolyet was thinking. "She has to people all that space, that silence, every day. You can't ask any more of her."

"Look here . . . she's really awfully good . . ."

The newspaper reporter could not take his eyes off her. This was one of the last rehearsals, and Jolyet was certain that Béatrice would be the revelation of the year, and perhaps a very great actress as well.

"Tell me something about her," the reporter was saying.

"She'll tell you herself, old man. I'm only the producer, you know."

The reporter smiled. They went everywhere together and it was common gossip that they were having an affair. For purely romantic reasons, Jolyet was waiting until the day of the preview to give substance to what people already were saying. Béatrice was impatient, because she found it healthier to have a lover. If he hadn't so definitely compromised her, she would never have forgiven him.

"How did you come to know her?"

"She'll tell you that, too. You'll find she's a good talker."

Indeed, Béatrice was perfect in her relations with the press. She answered questions in a manner, compounded of amiability and condescension, eminently fitted to a "lady of the stage." Fortunately she was not too well known; she had never been in moving pictures, and no scandal attached to her name. Now she came toward the two men, smiling, and Jolyet introduced the reporter to her.

"I'm going to the theater bar," he added. "I'll see you there later."

As he walked away, Béatrice's eyes followed him with a long look meant to reveal to the reporter what, actually, he already suspected. Then she turned graciously around, ready for the interview.

Half an hour later she joined Jolyet at the bar, clapped her hands in approval of his gin fizz, and ordered one for herself, which she drank through a straw. Every now and then she raised her head and looked at him out of her big, dark eyes.

Jolyet was touched. How appealing he found her, with

114

her offstage play-acting and her frantic little ambitions! How strange it was, in life's great circus, this will to succeed! He was tempted to be ironical about it.

"What vanity there is, dear Béatrice, in all these exertions we've been making!"

And he launched into a long harangue. This was one of his favorite diversions. He expatiated on something for ten minutes, she listened attentively, and then returned it to him in capsule form, thereby proving that she had taken in every bit of it. "After all," he would think, "if she can condense it so neatly, it must have called for condensation." To put the finger on his own mediocrity yielded him a sort of ferocious joy.

"Quite true," said Béatrice, when his little speech was over. "We don't amount to much. It's a good thing that usually we don't know it. Otherwise, we'd never do anything."

"Exactly!" Jolyet exulted. "Béatrice, you're perfect!"

And he kissed her hand. Béatrice decided that this was a good time to make certain things clear. Did he desire her, or was he a homosexual? Where a man was concerned, she could imagine no third way.

"André, do you know, there are some ugly rumors about you. I'm telling you because I'm your friend."

"What sort of rumors?"

"About your sexual inclinations," she said, lowering her voice.

He burst out laughing.

"And do you believe them? Dear Béatrice, how am I to put you straight?"

She knew right away that he was making fun of her. But before she could be angry, he held up his hand.

"You are very lovely, and very desirable. I hope that someday, very soon, you'll let me say more."

With regal dignity she held her hand out over the table, and on it he placed an amused kiss. Decidedly, he loved the theater.

Chapter 10

AT LAST the evening of the preview was at hand. In her dressing room, Béatrice looked with terror at the brocaded stranger in her glass. Her fate lay in this stranger's hands. Already she could hear the muffled sound of the audience's arrival, but for some reason she was perfectly cool and collected, and the expected stage fright did not come. All the best actors suffered from it, she knew, but she could only stand perfectly still and look at herself, repeating, quite mechanically, the first line she said in the play.

"What? Is he here again? Isn't it enough that I've obtained a pardon for him?"

No, she felt nothing at all, except for a slight dampness of her hands and an impression of absurdity. She had thought so often of this moment and struggled so hard to achieve it. She simply *must* succeed. Pulling herself together, she brushed back an unruly lock of hair.

"You're perfectly stunning!"

Jolyet, in his dinner jacket, had just opened the door. Smiling, he came up to her.

"What a shame that we have to be here! I should have liked to take you out dancing!"

"Have to be here," indeed! . . . Through the open door the noise was louder than before, and she became acutely conscious that "they" were waiting. She would be the object upon which their eyes converged, and later their tongues would wag about her. She was afraid. Taking Jolyet's hand, she squeezed it in her own. He was her partner, her accomplice, but he was going to leave her alone. For a moment she hated him.

"We must go down," he said.

Jolyet had planned the first scene in such a way that when the curtain went up Béatrice had her back to the audience. She was to be leaning on the piano and to turn around only after the minor character with whom she shared the stage had spoken twice. For this arrangement he had a very personal reason. He himself would be standing in the wings, where he could see the expression on her face when the curtain went up behind her. He was interested less in the success of the play than in the behavior of

118

the animal called Béatrice. And so now he put her in position and withdrew to his post in the wings.

The traditional three raps sounded, and Béatrice heard the rustle of the curtain. She was staring at an accidental fold in the piece of drapery thrown over the far end of the piano. Now "they" were looking at her. She stretched out a hand and flattened the drapery. Then what seemed to her like some other person wheeled around and said:

"What? Is he here again? Isn't it enough that I've obtained a pardon for him?"

That was over. She walked across the stage, forgetting that the leading man was a homosexual and also her sworn enemy, because he had a role no less important than hers. She was going to love him, and he must fall under her spell. His was the face of love. She was no longer aware of the dark, breathing mass beyond the stage at her right hand. Now, at last, she was really alive!

❋   ❋   ❋

Jolyet had seen the incident of the drapery. He had a fleeting premonition that one day Béatrice would make him suffer. Then, under the storm of applause that greeted the end of the first act, she came back to him, untouched and armed to the teeth, so that he could not but smile.

❋   ❋   ❋

The play was a triumph. Josée was delighted. She had always regarded Béatrice with a mixture of amusement and liking. Now she looked questioningly at Edouard, who was sitting beside her. He did not seem to be stirred too deeply. From the other side Jacques said:

"I'd rather go to the pictures any day, but it wasn't too bad."

Josée smiled at him, and he took her hand. Although she hated any public display of affection, she did not object. They had not seen each other for two whole weeks, because she had gone to visit her parents in Morocco. It was only this afternoon that he had called for her at the apartment of some friends, when his classes were over. From her seat in front of an open window, where she could enjoy the mild September air, she had seen him throw his coat down on a chair in the hall before hurrying to look for her. She had not moved, but she had felt an irrepressible smile come to her lips, and he had stopped short, smiling in the same half-agonized way. As he covered the few feet between them, she knew that she loved him. A big, burly fellow, hotheaded and not too bright, but she loved him just that way. When he had held her in his arms, very briefly because the friends were present, she had run her hands through his reddish hair, thinking: "I love him; yes, I do, and he loves me. I can't believe it." And ever since she had hardly dared breathe.

"Alain looks as if he were about to fall asleep," Edouard was saying.

After a lapse of three months, Alain had trembled at the prospect of seeing Béatrice again. But now he was stone cold. This beautiful and talented woman who was giving such a magnificent performance on the stage had no connection with him any more. His chief concern was how to get to his bar when the play was over. He was thirsty already. Bernard had quick-wittedly taken him out for a short nip of scotch in the first intermission, but when the second came around, Alain didn't have the courage to go again. Fanny wouldn't say a word, but he knew what she would be thinking. Anyhow, the lights were growing dim, and with a sigh he resigned himself to the third act.

* * *

It was wonderful; she had been told so over and over, and she knew it. And yet this assurance was of no use. Perhaps the next morning she would wake up with these words in her ear, and the certainty that she was Béatrice B . . . , the revelation of the season. But this evening. . . . She looked over at Jolyet, who was taking her home. He drove very slowly, with a reflective air.

"How does it feel to be a success?" he asked.

Béatrice did not answer. Success was the number of curious looks which she had faced during the supper after the preview, the exaggerated compliments pouring out of familiar faces, and the volley of questions that followed. The battle was won, and she marveled that the evidence of her victory should already be blown away.

They had reached the front door of her apartment house.

"May I come up?"

Jolyet was holding open the door of the car. Béatrice was dead tired, but she didn't dare say no. It was all quite logical, no doubt, but she could not find a connecting link between the will and ambition that had spurred her on so relentlessly ever since early youth, and this evening's fulfillment.

From her bed she watched Jolyet, in his shirt sleeves, pace up and down the room, discussing the play. It was just like him to maintain a passionate interest in the subject of a piece which he had chosen, produced, and then heard for three months in rehearsal.

"I'm thirsty," he concluded.

Béatrice pointed to the kitchen, and then watched him walk to it, with his narrow shoulders and excessively vivacious manner. For a moment she thought with regret of Edouard's long, sinuous body. She wished he, or someone his age, could be there to rave about the performance or else turn it to laughter, in other words, to re-endow it all with life of some kind. But there was only Jolyet, with his ironical remarks. And she must spend the night with him. Her eyes filled with tears, and suddenly she felt weak and very young. As the tears ran down her cheeks, she said to herself that everything was wonderful. Then Jolyet came back into the room. Fortunately Béatrice knew how to cry without spoiling her beauty.

She woke up in the middle of the night and thought at once of the preview. She did not think of her success; she thought of the three minutes after the curtain had been raised. After that she had turned around, and by this simple movement of her body she had overcome an enormous obstacle. Every evening, from now on, those three minutes would be exclusively hers. In confused fashion she guessed that they would turn out to be the only true minutes of her whole life, that such was her fate. Then she went peacefully back to sleep.

Chapter 11

THE following Monday evening the Maligrasses held one of their usual "at-homes," the first one since the preceding spring. Bernard and Nicole, the triumphantly modest Béatrice, Edouard, Jacques, and Josée were all there. Everyone had a very good time. Alain Maligrasse was a bit unsteady on his pins, but nobody noticed.

At one point Bernard found himself near Josée, leaning against a wall from which they could both watch the other people in the room. When he asked her a question, she pointed with her chin to the young musician, Fanny's protégé, who was just beginning to play the piano.

"I know that piece," Josée whispered. "It's very beautiful."

"It's just like last year. We were all of us here—do you remember?—and he played exactly the same thing. He can't have had any new ideas since. Neither have we, for that matter."

She made no reply, but looked at Jacques, who was at the other end of the room. Bernard followed her eyes.

"One day you won't love him any more," he said softly, "and one day I shan't love you, either. We'll find ourselves alone again, and nothing will have changed, except that another year will have gone by."

"I know," she answered.

In the shadows she took his hand and pressed it, without shifting her eyes back to his.

"Josée," he said, "it can't be like this. What have we done, all of us? What has happened? What does it all mean?"

"Don't think about it," she said tenderly. "If you do you'll go mad."